# OPPORTUNITIES

in

SO-AYC-113

# Restaurant Careers

## REVISED EDITION

**CAROL CAPRIONE CHMELYNSKI**

### VGM Career Books

Chicago   New York   San Francisco   Lisbon   London   Madrid   Mexico City
Milan   New Delhi   San Juan   Seoul   Singapore   Sydney   Toronto

**The McGraw·Hill** Companies

**Library of Congress Cataloging-in-Publication Data**

Chmelynski, Carol Ann Caprione.
     Opportunities in restaurant careers / Carol Ann Caprione Chmelynski
  — Rev. ed.
          p.     cm. (VGM opportunities series)
     ISBN 0-07-141165-8
     1. Food service—Vocational guidance—United States.     I. Title.     II. Series.

TX911.3.V62C46     2004
647.95′023′73—dc22                                       2003025820

1 2 3 4 5 6 7 8 9 0   LBM/LBM   3 2 1 0 9 8 7 6 5 4

ISBN 0-07-141165-8

Interior design by Rattray Design

McGraw-Hill books are available at special quantity discounts to use as premiums and sales promotions, or for use in corporate training programs. For more information, please write to the Director of Special Sales, Professional Publishing, McGraw-Hill, Two Penn Plaza, New York, NY 10121-2298. Or contact your local bookstore.

This book is printed on acid-free paper.

# CONTENTS

## 9. Educational Requirements and Resources

Opportunities in high school. Junior and community
colleges. Four-year universities or colleges. Training
in the restaurant industry.

# Foreword

THIS TRULY IS an exciting time to embark on a rewarding career within the restaurant and food-service industry. The nation's restaurants are an economic force providing not only substantial job opportunities for millions of individuals, but quality meals, service, and culinary options for American consumers every day.

In the last half-century, restaurants have become an essential part of the American lifestyle. They currently play an integral role in the nation's economy with direct sales of $426 billion and with an overall economic impact expected to exceed $1.2 trillion by 2004.

As the cornerstone of the economy, offering career opportunities and community involvement, the restaurant industry plays an invaluable role in society. There are 870,000 restaurant and food-service locations across the country, and the industry provides employment opportunities for 11.7 million employees of all ages and backgrounds, making the restaurant industry the largest employer outside of government.

With so many different sectors—including table service, quick service, institutional service, and catering, among others—making up this field, individuals possessing a wide range of talents can easily find success within the restaurant industry. Not surprisingly, eight out of ten salaried restaurant employees started as hourly employees, and salaries for food-service managers are growing at a rate twice as fast as the median salary for all managerial positions, clearly making the restaurant industry a gateway to success.

The industry continues to grow: by 2010 there will be more than a million restaurant locations generating sales of $577 billion, and by 2012 industry employment will reach 13.3 million.

The restaurant industry demonstrates its unwavering commitment to professionalism by cultivating, training, and continually educating its workforce. I wish you all the best as you strive for success in one of our country's most gratifying industries!

Steven C. Anderson
President and CEO
National Restaurant Association

# Overview of the Restaurant Industry

Restaurants play a vital role in today's society. They provide a convenience for busy two-career families and a means of entertainment for those who enjoy going out and having other people prepare and serve food to them. Restaurants were originally established as a necessary option for people who had to be away from home and couldn't use their own kitchens. Restaurants still serve that purpose, and today they help busy, overworked people who want to save time by eliminating the chores of food shopping, preparation, and cleanup. They are the cornerstone of our nation's economy, posting average sales of nearly $1.2 billion a day.

## Restaurant Types

There are many different types of eating establishments, including cafeterias, carryout operations, coffeehouses, drugstore counters, fast-food chains, sandwich shops, and white-tablecloth operations. A description of some of the different types of restaurants follows:

- **Family restaurant.** As the name implies, one would come to this restaurant with children, spouse, or friends for a casual meal in a relaxed, unpretentious atmosphere. Denny's, Red Lobster, and Pizza Hut are all examples of family restaurants.
- **Atmosphere restaurant.** The setting, decor, historic context, special artifacts, or view sets the atmosphere for this type of restaurant, which is usually visited for a special reason. The dress code is sometimes a little more formal than at a family restaurant. The Hard Rock Cafe restaurants, with their collections of memorabilia from the music world, are atmosphere restaurants.
- **Gourmet restaurant.** The food, service, and gracious atmosphere all add to a relaxed dining experience at this type of restaurant. It is more formal than the family or atmosphere restaurant, and it is characterized by an unhurried pace. Beer, wine, and liquor are offered. Often restaurants serving cuisines from other countries, such as France, Japan, and Italy, are gourmet restaurants.
- **Fast-food restaurant.** This type of restaurant primarily sells limited lines of beverages and prepared food items such as fish, hamburger, chicken, or roast beef sandwiches for consumption either on or near the premises or to take home. Fast-food restaurants are inexpensive, appeal to all ages, and are suitable for snack service as well as meal service. Seating is available, but customers are not served. Food is ordered and picked up at the counter. McDonald's and Burger King are two of the most successful fast-food restaurant chains.
- **Cafeterias.** Customers make food and beverage selections from a wide display of items. There may be some limited waiter or

waitress service. Tables and/or booths are usually provided. Ponderosa and Bonanza are two well-known cafeteria-style restaurant chains.

• **Take-out restaurant.** Food is purchased and taken off the premises—no seating is offered. Sometimes home delivery is available. Domino's Pizza is a take-out restaurant franchise.

• **Coffeehouses.** Once a gathering place for artists and intellectuals, this type of restaurant serves coffee and other refreshments to people who gather for conversation, games, or musical entertainment. Starbucks Coffee Company is one of the fastest-growing and most successful examples of a coffeehouse.

Keep in mind that these groupings are to some extent arbitrary, as restaurant categories rarely have neat, sharp boundaries. For example, the NDP CREST Association (food service industry specialists) breaks the commercial food service industry into the following three segments:

• **Quick-service segment.** Restaurants that fall under this category are perceived as fast-food or take-out restaurants. Patrons are generally not waited on in this type of restaurant. Instead, they may place orders at the drive through or counter, and either take the food out of the establishment or seat themselves at tables provided and eat indoors. Tips are minimal and not required. Foods typically served in this fashion are pizza, ice cream, chicken, or doughnuts.

• **Midscale segment.** Many restaurants fall into the midscale category. Patrons are shown to a table and a waiter or waitress takes the order and serves the food. Tips are required; usually reservations are not. Ruby Tuesday's, Bennigan's, and TGI Friday's are examples of midscale restaurants. These kinds of restaurants may, but are not required to, accept credit cards and serve beer, wine, or alcohol.

- **Upscale segment.** Restaurants in this category are not perceived as fast food/take out. Often reservations are necessary and sometimes a dress code is enforced. Elegance and leisure are goals of this type of restaurant. Credit cards are generally accepted and full liquor service, including beer, wine, and alcohol, is usually offered.

There are so many different kinds of dining establishments and restaurants because the very act of dining has become firmly established in the American culture as a thing to do, not only for nourishment, but also for enjoyment, fun, and leisure. When people eat out, they want a good experience, an interesting adventure, and an opportunity to try something new. Dinner in a restaurant—once just a prelude to a movie or the final social act after a play—has now become the theater. Dining out has become the show.

## Myriad Career Opportunities

The expanding importance of restaurants in American lifestyles is excellent news for those seeking a job in the restaurant industry. The following are ten good reasons to consider the restaurant industry when setting career goals.

1. The restaurant industry employs an estimated 11.7 million people, making it the nation's largest employer outside of government.
2. The restaurant industry ranks number one in the total number of business units.

3. The restaurant industry provides work for nearly 9 percent of those employed in the United States.

4. The restaurant industry continues to grow through both good and bad economic times.

5. Almost 54 billion meals are eaten in restaurants and school and work cafeterias each year.

6. Americans eat a meal or snack in restaurants an average of 5.4 times a week, or 280 times a year.

7. One-third of all adults in the United States have worked in the restaurant industry at some time during their lives.

8. In the United States, there are about 870,000 restaurant locations available to the public.

9. Total restaurant employment is expected to reach 13.3 million by 2012.

10. By 2010, the restaurant industry will operate more than one million units and post sales of $577 billion.

These facts about the restaurant industry can mean personal growth and opportunity for qualified, energetic people. That is why restaurant workers make up one of the largest and fastest-growing occupational groups in the nation's labor force. Indeed, job opportunities exist almost everywhere for almost any interested person, including those with limited skills and little formal education.

The restaurant industry is one of the very few industries today that still gives unskilled workers a chance to start at the bottom and work their way up. Of course, the amount of career preparation in both formal and on-the-job training determines the level of entry into the field. But restaurants have historically been workplaces that offer plenty of room for upward mobility, and people who are willing to make a personal investment in their success are practically guaranteed a good spot.

## Minority Management Opportunities

More than many other industries, the restaurant industry offers good managerial opportunities for women and minorities. According to the National Restaurant Association's website (restaurant .org), foodservice and lodging managers account for the largest number of managerial employees in the country, and eating-and-drinking places employ more minority managers than any other industry. The latest available figures on the NRA website also show the following:

- More than two-thirds (68 percent) of supervisors in food preparation and service occupations are women, 16 percent are African-American, and 13 percent are of Hispanic origin.
- Eating and drinking places rank second, based on sales volume, among retail establishments owned by African-Americans and Hispanics.
- The number of African-American-owned and women-owned eating-and-drinking establishments increased at double-digit rates between 1993 and 2003, with sales also rising dramatically.

## Traits for Succeeding in the Industry

A career in the restaurant industry can be one of the most rewarding, but it will also be one of the most demanding. People who are successful in the restaurant industry all possess several important qualities that contribute to their advancement. These qualities include:

- **Positive work attitudes.** These begin with punctuality, pride in personal appearance, and a professional manner. In addition, a good attitude means an eagerness to learn, a willingness to work, and an ability to accept constructive criticism and direction.

• **Intelligence and ambition.** The restaurant industry has a need and a place for people at all job levels. Therefore, opportunities to gain experience and on-the-job, as well as academic, training are excellent. Individuals who display the ambition to use these opportunities as stepping-stones to advancement and who also possess the intelligence to gain the maximum benefit from their training and experience are sure to succeed.

• **Physical and mental health.** Every restaurant job involves peak periods and deadlines leading up to them. Pressures can be intense; intermittent workloads can be heavy. Therefore, good physical health is a must. A healthy mental outlook that enables the individual to function well with fellow workers and serve the public effectively also is necessary.

## Growth in Good Times and Bad

Economic fluctuations can affect every industry, and the most noticeable effect of economic downturns on the restaurant industry has been a slowing in its rate of growth. That said, job prospects in this industry generally remain more healthy than most. For example, during recent economic downturns, restaurant sales volume as well as employment opportunities continued to rise.

The restaurant industry is one that offers excellent security potential for the long-term because it has almost always had more jobs than people to fill them. Its healthy growth performance indicates that this situation is likely to continue. Also, food is such a basic staple and food consumption away from home so vital to America's way of life that the industry is guaranteed a stable future as the nation's mobility and workforce grow.

## Employee Benefits

Currently the restaurant industry is experiencing a decrease in the available labor pool. This means there are more jobs available in the restaurant industry than there are people to perform those jobs. Because an eating establishment cannot operate without qualified employees, restaurant employers are offering higher salaries and more attractive benefit packages.

In many areas of the country, restaurant workers are reaping financial rewards as employers realize that the minimum wage is no longer a viable compensation to attract hard-working entry-level employees. In addition to competitive wages to hire and retain the most qualified workers, employers are now using benefit and incentive programs. In fact, many restaurants are accepting benefit and incentive programs as a required cost of doing business.

These incentive programs benefit both restaurant workers and employers. According to MDR Associates, a professional hospitality management consulting firm in Fairfax, Virginia, a properly organized and implemented benefit and incentive program can work as a marketing tool to help employers accomplish the following objectives:

- Attract and retain the most talented people for the organization
- Improve overall employee relations
- Increase employee morale, motivation, and performance
- Reduce employee absenteeism from the job
- Reduce overtime hours necessary because of absenteeism
- Decrease employee turnover
- Generate cost savings because less time is spent on training new staff

Benefit and incentive programs offered to restaurant employees can vary from operation to operation. Some of the more common benefits offered include the following:

- **Medical and health-related programs.** Included in such programs are hospital, surgical, accident, and major medical and dental insurance plans. Sometimes additional health programs are administered by the employer to include contributory payments for those items not covered by the standard plans, such as physical examinations, clinic visits, routine dental services, vision and auditory exams, and blood-bank usage costs.
- **Insurance programs.** Group life, individual life, accidental death/dismemberment, long- and short-term disability, and travel-accident policies are common benefits for older, management-level employees.
- **Additional pay programs.** Overtime, extra shifts, and/or holiday, sick, and vacation pay come under this heading.
- **Educational assistance.** Operations that require large numbers of young workers have found educational assistance to be a very effective employee lure. An educational assistance program might include tuition aid contributions or scholarship awards for those employees attending or planning to attend college.

Education programs that are aimed at increasing an employee's knowledge of his or her current job or of the overall industry benefit both the employer and the employee. On-the-job training programs, attendance at local industry seminars, and paid subscriptions to industry journals are also common examples of benefits in this area.

- **Employee counseling.** Some restaurants participate in referral counseling programs such as alcohol/drug assistance, personal/emotional counseling, financial/credit management assistance, legal services, and preretirement counseling.

• **Child care.** Because private child-care facilities are too expensive for all but the largest corporate organizations, small or independent restaurant operators who recognize the increasing role that working mothers play in the restaurant industry workforce have implemented a variety of programs to assist the parents on their staffs. These benefits include referral programs to nearby licensed child-care centers, contributions to child-care costs, flexible hours and/or responsibilities for those workers who must provide transportation to and from day-care centers, sick-child days given as personal and unpaid leave time without affecting seniority or accrual of benefits, and maternity and paternity leave after the birth of a child, again without compromising seniority.

• **Performance incentives.** The most cost-effective benefit and incentive program is a system of awards and bonuses given for desired performance. These performance incentives can take the form of length-of-service awards, idea/suggestion box awards, productivity awards, and safety commendations.

• **Profit sharing.** Probably one of the greatest performance incentives is profit sharing. Companies using a profit-sharing plan have reported that it has resulted in measurable benefits, such as a decrease in absenteeism, tardiness, and turnover and an increase in productivity, employee interest, and effort. Profit sharing also encourages acceptance of change and new technology and, in fact, any action that might increase profits. It also promotes teamwork among employees, management, and stockholders by providing a single objective for unified attention.

In addition, a number of restaurants offer the following benefits and incentives:

• Bereavement leave and pay
• Christmas party

- Coffee breaks
- Corporate membership
- Credit union memberships
- Direct deposit of payroll checks
- Discounts to employee family members
- Flexible hours
- Health club membership
- Holiday turkey or ham
- Jury duty leave
- Locker room/shower facilities
- Meal allowances
- Parking cost assistance
- Recreational activities
- Relocation expense reimbursement
- Safety commendations
- Summer picnic
- Trade journals and periodicals
- Transportation cost assistance
- Uniform/dry cleaning allowance
- Vending machines
- Well-pay programs

# The Future of the Restaurant Industry

What will the restaurant industry be like in the near future? To help restaurant operators answer this question, the National Restaurant Association embarked on a futuristic study to develop a snapshot of the restaurant industry in the year 2010.

By employing the Delphi approach—a research method that uses a panel of industry experts to identify and analyze issues by subjective judgments rather than precise analytical techniques—the NRA study provides a unique glimpse of the restaurant industry a few years into the future. This survey is intended to aid restaurant operators in planning efforts. It will also provide helpful insights to those individuals who are considering a career in the restaurant industry.

The following details some of the findings of the NRA's survey "Restaurant Industry 2010: The Road Ahead."

## Industry Structure in 2010

More demanding customers and ever-increasing competition will require enhanced operational excellence from restaurateurs in the next decade.

The restaurant industry is poised for growth. Today's consumers spend 44 percent of every food dollar on meals, snacks, and beverages purchased away from home, up from just 25 percent in 1955. By 2010, panelists estimate the figure will reach 53 percent. In addition, by 2010, the Delphi panelists predict international expansion of U.S restaurant companies will grow tenfold.

Chains will continue to increase their share of the market, diversifying their offerings through multiple concepts. Despite chain growth, panelists say, independent restaurateurs will still be the leading innovators and new product developers.

Takeout and delivery will capture a greater proportion of total industry sales as restaurateurs fulfill consumers' ever-increasing need for convenience. But on-premise dining will enjoy growth as well, particularly casual, ethnic, family style, and theme restaurants.

### The Role of Technology

Today's restaurateurs are just beginning to explore the implications of high-technology solutions. Technological advances will allow operators to more easily monitor profit and loss on a daily basis.

Technology will also help restaurateurs more effectively control costs and enhance management efficiency.

By 2010, panelists say, the successful restaurateurs will be the ones who readily incorporate high-tech applications into everyday operations while remaining people oriented. The challenge for restaurateurs will be to combine their people-orientation skills with high-tech skills, becoming both high tech and high touch.

### Higher Expectations

As competition continues to intensify, patrons will expect higher levels of service and food quality, both on and off the premises.

Tomorrow's customer will be less forgiving and expect restaurateurs to deliver higher-quality take-out food. To accommodate this more demanding customer, restaurateurs will put suppliers under increased pressure to improve food quality and food safety.

## *The Workforce in 2010*

By 2010, a greater proportion of the industry's workforce will come from culturally diverse immigrant populations. This diversity will require management to foster an atmosphere of cooperation and accommodation within the restaurant workplace.

As the baby boom population ages, older workers will be more commonplace in the restaurant industry. Also, more women and minorities will move into upper management positions.

### A More Skilled Workforce

By 2010, the restaurant industry will demand that prospective employees have better skills in keeping with the requirements needed to operate and maintain high-tech equipment; the industry will also be seeking more highly educated managers.

Hotel, restaurant, and institutional (HRI) schools will be turning out more graduates as programs expand and more schools establish HRI programs.

Because growth might easily be curtailed by lack of staff, restaurant employers will focus more attention than ever on training and retaining employees. Training and communications will be key factors in retention of hourly employees. Management training will focus on managing a diverse workforce and solving problems. Certification will become increasingly important for all employees.

## Compensation and Benefits

To attract qualified employees, the industry will become more competitive in compensation and benefits. In response to workers' demands for more free time and a better family lifestyle, the industry will offer such benefits as child care as well as a shorter work-week, limiting management to fifty hours per week.

## *Healthier Food Preparation*

By 2010, more restaurant menus will offer low-fat and vegetarian or low-cholesterol foods. Because taste will continue to be the motivating factor in food choices, restaurants will need to become more involved in testing recipes. Customers will expect great tasting dishes that are "good for you."

Health-conscious patrons will be paying increased attention to calories and fat grams when selecting food items. Main-dish salads with a choice of grilled toppings will be standard menu offerings, along with vegetarian items.

The panelists predict a significant upgrade in product and an emphasis on "fresh" at midscale restaurants, as well as a greater demand for authentic items and flavor profiles. Continuing today's trend, menu items will be spicier and more pungent to the taste. Also, panelists predict, restaurants will serve more wine, offer better wine lists, and include organic wines.

## *Ease and Sanitation*

By 2010, much of the kitchen equipment will be on wheels for ease of movement and will have quick disconnect systems for easier cleaning and flexibility.

In terms of sanitation, more restaurants will rely on cleaning without chemicals, and more will require their own internal water purification systems—both of which are driven by the upswing in environmental awareness and concerns.

# 2

## ENTRY-LEVEL RESTAURANT WORKERS

THE RESTAURANT INDUSTRY is rare in that it offers a wide range of opportunities to people at all levels of educational attainment. Almost any interested person, including people who have limited skills or little formal education, can find a niche in this growing industry.

The industry has opportunities for working people of virtually all ages. For sixteen-year-old high school students or for those who are beginning or changing a career later in life, a career in the restaurant industry can prove to be an excellent choice.

## Jobs Requiring Minimal Training

Many job opportunities exist in the food-service industry for people who have no previous job experience. In fact, nearly two out of three food counter and fountain workers and almost 20 percent of all chefs, cooks, and food preparation workers are sixteen to nineteen years of age. In this section, you'll learn about a range of different positions requiring little to no additional education; these are excellent choices for entry-level work, for those with few transferable skills, and for those looking to establish a history of employment.

## *Bus Persons*

Bus persons clear and reset tables with fresh linen and silverware, refill water glasses, and assist waiters and waitresses with serving and housekeeping chores in the dining area. Many people who now enjoy high-level management positions in the restaurant industry began their careers as bus persons. This is a good job to get started in the restaurant industry. Employers risk little in hiring a bus person and may promote accordingly if the employee shows a strong work ethic and reliability.

## *Waiters and Waitresses*

The largest group of food-service workers is made up of waiters and waitresses. They take customers' orders, serve food and beverages, prepare itemized checks, and sometimes accept payment. However, the manner in which they perform these tasks varies considerably, depending on the type of restaurant establishment in which they work. In coffee shops, for example, they are expected to provide fast and efficient, yet courteous, service.

In fine restaurants, where gourmet meals are accompanied by attentive formal service, waiters and waitresses serve the meal at a more leisurely pace and offer more personal service to patrons. For example, they might recommend a certain kind of wine as a complement to a particular entrée, explain how menu items are prepared, or complete preparations on some salads and other special dishes right at the table.

Depending on the type of restaurant, waiters and waitresses might be required to perform duties associated with other food and beverage service occupations in addition to waiting on tables. Some of these tasks might include escorting guests to tables, serving customers seated at counters, setting up and clearing tables, or operating the cash register. However, in larger or more formal restaurants, waiters and waitresses usually are not required to perform these duties.

Waiters and waitresses are critical to any type of restaurant because they are the "face" of the restaurant—they interact with the customers. They must like people and be pleasant, poised, and efficient under the stress of simultaneous demands.

## *Hosts and Hostesses*

Hosts and hostesses are responsible for evoking a good impression of the restaurant by warmly welcoming guests. In a courteous manner, they direct patrons to where they may leave their coats and other personal items and show patrons where they should wait until their table is ready. Hosts and hostesses assign guests to tables suitable for the size of their group, escort them to their seats, and provide menus.

As restaurants' personal representatives to patrons, hosts and hostesses must try to ensure that service is prompt and courteous and the meal is enjoyable. They also ensure order and cleanliness and address any complaints dissatisfied diners might have. Hosts and hostesses schedule dining reservations, arrange parties, and organize any special services that are required. In some restaurants, they also perform cashier duties.

## Sanitation/Maintenance Employees

Sanitation/maintenance employees ensure that walls and floors are clean and that there is a steady flow of clean cooking equipment, utensils, dishware, and silverware. Most modern restaurants have dishwashers and other machines to assist in performing these tasks. Although the job does not sound glamorous, sanitation and maintenance employees are vital to the operation of any restaurant.

## Dining Room Attendants and Bartenders' Assistants

Dining room attendants and bartenders' assistants help waiters, waitresses, and bartenders by keeping the serving area stocked with supplies, by cleaning tables, and by removing dirty dishes. They replenish the supply of clean linen, dishes, silverware, and glasses in the restaurant dining room and keep the bar stocked with glasses, liquor, ice, and drink garnishes. Bartenders' helpers also keep the bar equipment clean and wash glasses. Dining room attendants set tables with clean tablecloths, napkins, silverware, glasses, and dishes and serve ice water, rolls, and butter to patrons.

At the end of the meal, dining room attendants remove dirty dishes and linens from the tables and take them to the kitchen. Cafeteria attendants stock serving tables with food, trays, dishes, and silverware and carry trays to dining tables for patrons.

## Counter Attendants

Counter attendants take orders and serve food at counters. In cafeterias, they serve food displayed on counters and steam tables as requested by patrons, carve meat, dish out vegetables, ladle sauces and soups, and fill cups and glasses.

In lunchrooms and coffee shops, counter attendants take orders from customers seated at the counter, transmit the orders to the kitchen, and pick up and serve the food when it is ready. They also fill cups and glasses with coffee, soda, and other beverages and prepare fountain specialties such as milk shakes and ice-cream sundaes. Often counter attendants prepare short-order items such as sandwiches and salads and wrap or place orders in containers to be taken out and consumed elsewhere. In addition, counter attendants write up itemized checks and accept payment.

### Fast-Food Workers

Fast-food workers take orders from customers standing at counters at fast-food restaurants. They gather the ordered beverage and food items from the stock waiting to be sold, serve them to the customer, and accept payment. Many fast-food workers also cook and package french fries, make coffee, and fill beverage cups using a drink-dispensing machine. These workers must be fast, friendly, and efficient. They should be good at multitasking and know how to handle simple math as they accept money and make change for orders.

## Working Conditions

Restaurant workers are on their feet most of the time and often have to carry heavy trays of food, dishes, and glassware. During busy dining periods, they are under pressure to serve customers quickly and efficiently. The work is relatively safe, but care must be taken to avoid slips and falls or burns.

Although some restaurant employees work forty hours or more a week, the majority of employees work part-time—a larger proportion than in almost any other occupation. The majority of those working part-time schedules do so on a voluntary basis because the wide range in dining hours creates work opportunities attractive to homemakers, students, and others in need of supplemental income.

Many restaurant workers are expected to work evenings, weekends, and holidays. Some choose to work split shifts, meaning they work several hours during the middle of the day, take a few hours off in the afternoon, and then return to their jobs in the evening.

## Employment

Recent figures indicate the great number of jobs held by restaurant workers. Combined food preparation and serving workers hold approximately 2.2 million of these jobs; waiters and waitresses, 2 million; dishwashers, 525,000; dining room and cafeteria attendants and bartender helpers, 431,000; counter attendants, 421,000; and hosts and hostesses, 343,000.

Restaurants, coffee shops, bars, and other retail eating and drinking places employed the overwhelming majority of all food and beverage service workers. Of the remainder, nearly half worked in hotels and other lodging places. Others worked in bowling alleys, casinos, country clubs, and other membership organizations.

Jobs are located throughout the country but are most plentiful in large cities and tourist areas. Vacation resorts offer seasonal employment, and some workers alternate between summer and winter resorts instead of remaining in one area the entire year.

## Training

There are no specific educational requirements for restaurant jobs. Although many employers prefer to hire high school graduates for waiter and waitress and host and hostess positions, a high school degree is usually not required for fast-food workers, counter attendants, and dining room attendants and bartenders' helpers. Many entrants to these jobs have little or no work experience.

More important are the skills and traits you possess. You should stress your problem-solving, multitasking, and people skills to your potential employer.

## Other Qualifications

Restaurant employers place a high emphasis on personal qualities. Restaurant workers should be well spoken and have a neat and clean appearance because they are in close contact with the public. They should enjoy dealing with all kinds of people. A pleasant disposition and a sense of humor are important. State laws often require that restaurant workers obtain health certificates showing that they are free of contagious diseases.

Waiters and waitresses need a good memory to avoid confusing customers' orders and to recall the faces, names, and preferences of frequent patrons. They also should be good at arithmetic if they have to total bills without the aid of a calculator or cash register. In restaurants specializing in ethnic foods, a foreign language is helpful.

Experience waiting on tables is preferred by restaurants and hotels that have rigid table service standards. Jobs at these establishments often have higher earnings but might also require higher educational standards than less formal establishments.

Most restaurant workers acquire their skills on the job by observing and working with more experienced workers. Some employers, particularly in some fast-food restaurants, use self-instruction programs to teach new employees food-preparation and service skills through the use of audiovisual presentations and instructional booklets.

Some public and private vocational schools, restaurant associations, and large restaurant chains provide classroom training in a generalized food-service curriculum.

## Advancement

Opportunities for advancement are limited in small restaurant establishments. After gaining some experience, some dining room and cafeteria attendants and bartenders' helpers are able to advance to waiter, waitress, or bartender jobs.

Waiters and waitresses often advance by finding a job in a larger restaurant where prospects for tips are better. Some hosts and hostesses and waiters and waitresses advance to supervisory jobs, such as maître d'hotel, dining room supervisor, or restaurant manager. In larger restaurant chains, those who excel at their jobs often are invited to enter the company's management training program.

## Job Outlook

Job openings for restaurant workers are expected to be abundant through 2010, stemming from increases in population, personal incomes, and leisure time. While employment growth will produce many new jobs, most openings will come from the need to replace the high proportion of workers who leave this occupation each year. There is substantial movement into and out of these occupations because the minimal education and training requirements for these jobs allow easy entry, and the predominance of part-time jobs is attractive to persons seeking a short-term source of income rather than a career. However, keen competition is expected for food servers in popular restaurants and fine dining establishments, where potential earnings from tips are greatest.

Projected employment growth of restaurant workers will vary by type of job through 2010. Employment of fast-food workers is expected to increase faster than average in response to the continuing fast-paced lifestyle of many Americans and the addition of healthier foods in many fast-food restaurants. Increases in the number of families and the more affluent fifty-five-and-older population will result in more restaurants that offer table service and more varied menus—leading to fast as average growth for waiters and waitresses and hosts and hostesses. A decline is expected in the employment of dining room attendants, as waiters and waitresses increasingly assume their duties.

Potential earnings are highest in popular restaurants and fine dining establishments. Therefore, these restaurants will experience keen competition for a limited number of jobs.

## Earnings

Restaurant workers derive their earnings from a combination of hourly wages and customer tips. Their wages and the amount of tips they receive vary greatly, depending on the type of job and the establishment.

For example, fast-food workers and hosts and hostesses generally do not receive tips, so their wage requirement might be higher than that of waiters and waitresses, who might earn more from tips than from wages. In some restaurants, these workers contribute a portion of their tips to a pool, which is distributed among many of the establishment's other food and beverage service workers. This arrangement allows workers who normally do not receive tips, such as dishwashers, to share in the rewards for a room well served.

Median hourly earnings (not including tips) of waiters and waitresses average $6.42. The middle 50 percent earns between $5.88 and $7.26; the top 10 percent earns more than $10.15 per hour. For most waiters and waitresses, higher earnings are primarily the result of receiving more in tips rather than higher hourly wages. Tips usually average between 10 and 20 percent of guests' checks, so waiters and waitresses working in busy, expensive restaurants earn the highest wages.

Median hourly earnings (not including tips) of full-time dining room attendants and bartender's helpers average about $6.53. The middle 50 percent earns between $5.97 and $7.62. The top 10 percent earns more than $9.26 an hour. Most receive over half of their earnings as wages; the rest is their share of the proceeds from tip pools.

Median hourly earnings of counter attendants in cafeterias, food concession, and coffee shops (not including tips) average $6.72. The middle 50 percent earns between $6.07 and $8.05 an hour, while the highest 10 percent earns more than $9.92 an hour. Although some counter attendants receive part of their earnings as tips, fast-food workers generally do not.

Federal law permits employers to credit an employee's tip earnings toward the minimum hourly wage up to an amount equaling 45 percent of minimum wage. Some employers exercise this right. Employers are also permitted to deduct from wages the cost, or fair value, of any meals or lodging provided. However, many employers provide free meals and furnish uniforms. Restaurant workers who work full-time often receive paid vacation, sick leave, and health insurance; part-time workers generally do not.

# 3

# MIDLEVEL POSITIONS

IN THE RESTAURANT industry, job positions in the midlevel category vary considerably from one establishment to another. Generally, these positions require some experience, involve greater amounts of responsibility, and often garner better wages than those of entry-level positions. On-the-job training is usually provided for the recently hired. This chapter offers an overview of various midlevel positions.

## Bartenders

Bartenders must be able to skillfully prepare a drink at a moment's notice. It might be a cool glass of gin and tonic or a colorful, exotic mixture such as a Singapore Sling. Bartenders make these drinks by combining, in exact proportions, ingredients selected from what might seem to be a bewildering variety of alcoholic beverages, mixes, and garnishes. A well-stocked bar contains dozens of types and brands of liquor, beer, and wine plus soft drinks, fruits and fruit juices, cream, soda, and tonic water.

Bartenders fill the drink orders that waiters and waitresses take from customers seated in the restaurant or lounge as well as orders from customers seated at the bar. Because some people like their cocktails made a specific way, bartenders occasionally are asked to mix drinks to suit customers' tastes. Most bartenders are required to know dozens of drink recipes and to be able to mix drinks accurately, quickly, and without waste, even during the busiest periods. Therefore, an excellent memory is important.

Besides mixing and serving drinks, bartenders collect payment, operate the cash register, and clean up after customers have left. They also may serve food items to customers seated at the bar.

Bartenders who work at service bars have little contact with customers. They work at small bars in restaurants, hotels, and clubs where drinks are served only to diners at tables. However, the majority of bartenders work in eating and drinking establishments where they also directly serve and socialize with patrons.

Many establishments, especially larger ones, use automatic equipment to mix drinks of varying complexity at the push of a button. However, bartenders still must be efficient and knowledgeable so they can prepare drinks not handled by the automatic equipment or mix drinks if the equipment is not functioning. Also, equipment is no substitute for the friendly socializing most customers prefer and expect.

Bartenders usually are responsible for ordering and maintaining an inventory of liquor, mixers, and other bar supplies. They also arrange the bottles and glassware into attractive displays and often wash glassware used at the bar.

### Working Conditions

Many bartenders work more than forty hours per week; night work, weekend work, and split shifts are common. For many bartenders, however, the opportunity for friendly conversation with customers and the possibility of one day managing or owning a bar or restaurant of their own more than offset these disadvantages. For others, the opportunity to be able to have only part-time employment is important.

Because bartenders play a significant role in making an establishment attractive to customers, a pleasant, outgoing personality is a must in this career. In addition to understanding and liking all kinds of people, bartenders must have excellent memories for faces, names, and recipes. Many bartenders pride themselves on being able to fill any drink order without looking up a recipe and are able to mix and serve drinks with flair, a quality that helps make them popular with customers and employees alike.

Good bartenders must be able to work accurately and rapidly. Busy periods in popular establishments can create considerable pressure, making a cool efficiency, as well as attention to detail, an occupational necessity.

Because bartenders are required to stand for many hours, good physical condition is vital. Better-than-average strength is sometimes needed to lift heavy cases of liquor or mixes.

Generally, bartenders must be at least twenty-one years of age, and employers prefer to hire persons who are twenty-five or older. Bartenders also should be familiar with state and local laws concerning the sale of alcoholic beverages.

## Training

Some bartenders acquire their skills by attending a bartending school or taking vocational and technical school courses that include instruction on state and local laws and regulations, cocktail recipes, attire and conduct, and stocking a bar. Some of these schools help their graduates find jobs.

## Earnings

Median hourly earnings (not including tips) of bartenders average $6.86. The middle 50 percent earns between $6.10 and $8.44. The highest 10 percent earns more than $11.14. Like waiters and waitresses, bartenders employed in public bars may receive more than half of their earnings in tips. Service bartenders are often paid higher hourly wages to offset their lower tip earnings.

# Chefs, Cooks, and Other Kitchen Workers

Cooks and chefs are the artists and the administrators of the restaurant industry. These people perform some of the most creative and interesting jobs of the entire industry. There is a strong demand for talented, well-trained cooks and chefs throughout the country.

Recent statistics show that more than 2.8 million chefs and cooks and other kitchen workers are working in restaurants and other eating establishments. Job openings for these workers are expected to be plentiful through 2010.

## Nature of the Work

In any restaurant—whether it prides itself on home cooking or exotic foreign cuisine—chefs, cooks, and other kitchen workers largely are responsible for the reputation it acquires.

Some restaurants are famous for offering a varied menu featuring meals that are time-consuming and difficult to prepare. These restaurants demand a highly skilled chef. Other restaurants emphasize fast service and offer hamburgers and sandwiches that can be prepared in advance or even in a few minutes by a fast-food or short-order cook who has only limited cooking skills.

Chefs and cooks are responsible for preparing meals that are tasty and attractively presented. Although the terms *chef* and *cook* are often used interchangeably, the professional chef generally is a far more skilled, trained, and experienced individual.

Many chefs have earned fame for themselves and the restaurants, hotels, and institutions where they work because of their skill in artfully preparing the traditional favorites as well as creating new dishes and improving familiar ones.

Institutional chefs and cooks work in the kitchens of schools, industrial cafeterias, hospitals, and other institutions. For each meal, they prepare a small selection of entrées, vegetables, and desserts, but in large quantities and in huge kettles, not small pots. Restaurant chefs and cooks generally prepare a wider selection of dishes for each meal, cooking most individual servings to order.

Whether they work in institutions or in restaurants, chefs and cooks measure, mix, and cook ingredients according to recipes. They use a variety of pots, pans, cutlery, and equipment including ovens, broilers, grills, slicers, grinders, and blenders in the course of their work.

In addition, chefs and cooks often are responsible for directing the work of other kitchen workers, estimating food requirements, and ordering food supplies. Some chefs and cooks also help plan meals and develop menus.

Bread and pastry bakers, called pastry chefs in some kitchens, produce baked goods for restaurants, institutions, and retail bakery shops. Unlike bakers, who work at large automated industrial bakeries, bread and pastry bakers need only supply the customers who visit their establishment. They bake smaller quantities of breads, rolls, pastries, pies, and cakes, doing most of the work by hand. They measure and mix ingredients, shape and bake the dough, and apply fillings and decorations.

Short-order cooks prepare foods to order in restaurants and coffee shops that specialize in fast service. They grill and garnish hamburgers, prepare sandwiches, fry eggs, and cook french fries, often working on several orders at the same time. Prior to busy periods, short-order cooks might slice meats and cheese or prepare coleslaw or potato salad. During slow periods, they might clean the grill as well as other food preparation surfaces and the counter. In small establishments, such as diners, short-order cooks may serve people at the counter, collect payments, and operate the cash register.

Specialty fast-food cooks are responsible for preparing a limited selection of menu items in fast-food restaurants. They cook and package batches of food such as hamburgers and fried chicken, which are prepared to order or kept warm until sold.

Other kitchen workers, under the direction of chefs and cooks, are responsible for performing tasks that require less skill. Their duties include weighing and measuring ingredients, fetching pots and pans, and stirring and straining soups and sauces. They clean; peel and slice potatoes, vegetables, and fruits; and make salads. They also might have to cut and grind meats, poultry, and seafood in preparation for cooking. They clean work areas, equipment, and utensils as well as dishes and silverware.

The number and types of workers employed in the kitchen depend partly on the size and kind of restaurant. Fast-food outlets offer only a few items, which are prepared by fast-food cooks. Smaller restaurants usually feature a limited number of easy-to-prepare items, supplemented by short-order specialties and ready-made desserts. Usually one chef or cook prepares all the food with the help of a short-order cook and one or two other kitchen workers.

Large eating places usually have more varied menus and prepare, from start to finish, more of the food they serve. Kitchen staffs often include several chefs or cooks, sometimes called assistant or apprentice chefs or cooks, a bread and pastry baker, and many less skilled kitchen workers. Each cook or chef usually has a special assignment and often a special job title such as vegetable, fry, or sauce cook.

Executive chefs or head cooks coordinate the work of the kitchen staff and often direct certain kinds of food preparation. They decide the serving sizes, plan the menus, and buy the food supplies.

## Working Conditions

Many restaurant and institutional kitchens have modern equipment, convenient work areas, and air-conditioning; but others, particularly older and smaller eating establishments, are not so well equipped. Other variations in working conditions depend on the type and quantity of food being prepared and the local laws governing food-service operations.

Workers generally are required to withstand the pressure and strain of working in close quarters during busy periods, stand for hours at a time, lift heavy pots and kettles, and work near hot ovens and ranges. Job hazards might include falls, cuts, and burns, but injuries are seldom serious.

Work hours in restaurants might include late evening, holiday, and weekend work, while hours in cafeterias in factories, schools, or other institutions may be more regular. Kitchen workers employed by public and private schools may work during the school year only, usually for nine or ten months. Vacation resorts offer seasonal employment.

## Employment

Statistics show that chefs, cooks, and other kitchen workers hold approximately 2.8 million jobs. Short-order and fast-food cooks hold 727,000 of the jobs, restaurant cooks 668,000, institution and cafeteria cooks 465,000, chefs and head cooks 139,000, and other kitchen workers 849,200.

Almost 60 percent of all chefs, cooks, and other kitchen workers work in restaurants and other retail food-service establishments. About 20 percent work in institutions such as schools, universities, prisons, hospitals, and nursing homes. Hotels, grocery stores, government and factory cafeterias, private clubs, and many other organizations employ the remainder. More than one-third work part-time.

## Training

Most kitchen workers start as fast-food or short-order cooks or in one of the other less skilled kitchen positions that require little education or training and that allow them to acquire their skills on the job. After gaining some basic food-handling, preparation, and cooking skills, they might be able to advance to an assistant cook or short-order cook.

However, many years of training and experience are necessary to achieve the level of skill required of an executive chef or cook in a fine restaurant. Even though a high school diploma is not required for beginning jobs, it is highly recommended for those planning a career as a cook or chef. High school or vocational school courses in business, mathematics, and business administration are particularly helpful.

An ever-increasing number of chefs and cooks are obtaining their training through high school or post–high school vocational programs and two- or four-year colleges. Chefs and cooks might also be trained in apprenticeship programs offered by professional culinary institutes, industry associations, and trade unions. An example is the three-year apprenticeship program administered by local chapters of the American Culinary Federation in cooperation with local employers and junior colleges or vocational education institutions. In addition, some large hotels and restaurants operate their own training programs for new employees.

Persons who have had courses in commercial food preparation may be able to start as a cook or chef without having to spend time in a lower-skilled kitchen job, and they may have an advantage when looking for jobs in better restaurants and hotels, where hiring standards often are more demanding. Some high school vocational programs offer food preparation training; however, these courses, which range from a few months to two years or more and in some cases are open only to high school graduates, usually are offered by trade schools, vocational centers, colleges, professional associations, and trade unions. The armed forces also are a good source of training and experience.

Curricula vary, but cooking students usually learn their craft by actually broiling, baking, and otherwise preparing food. They also learn how to use and care for kitchen equipment. Training programs often include instruction in menu planning, determining portion size, controlling food costs, purchasing food supplies in quantity, selecting and storing food, and using leftover food to minimize waste. Students also learn hotel and restaurant sanitation and public health rules regarding food handling.

Training in supervisory and management skills sometimes is emphasized in courses offered by private vocational schools, professional associations, and university programs.

Many school districts, in cooperation with school services divisions of state departments of education, provide on-the-job training and sometimes summer workshops for cafeteria kitchen workers who wish to become cooks. Junior colleges, community colleges, and culinary schools also offer training programs. (See Appendixes A and B.)

Certification provides valuable formal recognition of the skills of a chef or cook. The American Culinary Federation certifies chefs and cooks at the levels of cook, chef, pastry chef, executive chef, and master chef. Certification standards are based primarily on experience and formal training.

### Other Qualifications

The ability to work as part of a team, a keen sense of taste and smell, and personal cleanliness are important qualities for chefs, cooks, and other kitchen workers. Most states require health certificates indicating that these workers are free from contagious diseases.

### Advancement

Advancement opportunities for chefs and cooks are better than for most other food and beverage preparation and service occupations. Many acquire higher paying positions and new cooking skills by moving from one job to another. Others gradually advance to executive chef positions, particularly in hotels, clubs, or larger, more elegant restaurants.

Some chefs and cooks eventually go into business as caterers or restaurant owners; others might become instructors in vocational programs in high schools, junior and community colleges, and other academic institutions.

### Job Outlook

Employment openings for chefs, cooks, and other kitchen workers are expected to be plentiful through 2010. Employment growth will create many job openings, but most openings will arise from the need to replace the relatively high proportion of workers who leave this very large occupation each year.

There is substantial turnover in many of these jobs because the limited formal education and training requirements allow easy entry, and the large number of part-time positions is attractive to persons seeking a short-term source of income rather than a career. Workers under the age of twenty-five have traditionally filled a significant proportion of these jobs. Many of the workers who leave these jobs transfer to other occupations; others stop working to assume household responsibilities or to attend school full-time. Many employers will be forced to offer higher wages, better fringe benefits, and more training to attract and retain workers.

Employment of chefs, cooks, and other kitchen workers is expected to increase about as fast as the average for all occupations through 2010. Because the overall level of economic activity affects restaurant food and beverage sales, sales and employment will increase with the growth of the economy.

Other factors contributing to employment growth will be population growth, rising family and personal incomes, and more leisure time that will allow people to dine out and take vacations more often. Also, as more women join the workforce, families increasingly may find dining out a welcome convenience.

Employment in restaurants is expected to grow. Increasing demand for restaurants that offer table service and varied menus, particularly more expensive restaurants that offer more exotic foods, will require more highly skilled cooks and chefs.

Employment in cafeterias in educational and health services is expected to increase more slowly than the average. Many high schools and hospitals are trying to make "institutional food" more attractive by employing highly trained chefs and cooks to prepare more appealing meals; others are contracting out their food services.

## *Earnings*

According to the latest figures available, many executive chefs earn more than $50,000 a year. Median hourly earnings of cooks are $8.72 and generally range between $6.30 and $12.43. Median hourly earnings of cooks in fast-food restaurants are $6.53.

Short-order cooks have median hourly earnings of $7.55; most earn between $6.32 and $9.20. Median hourly earnings of institution and cafeteria cooks are $8.22; most earn within the range of $6.70 to $10.24. Food preparation workers generally earn less, with median hourly earnings of $7.38; most earn between $6.28 and $8.81.

Wages of chefs, cooks, and other kitchen workers vary depending on the part of the country and especially the type of establishment in which they work. Wages generally are highest in elegant restaurants and hotels. Some employers provide uniforms and free meals, but federal law permits employers to deduct from wages the cost, or fair value, of any meals or lodging provided, and some employers exercise this right. Chefs, cooks, and food preparation workers who work full-time often receive typical benefits, but part-time workers usually do not.

# 4

# MANAGEMENT POSITIONS

THERE ARE MANY different kinds of management positions available in the restaurant industry. Some positions are concerned with specific tasks, while others are set up in such a way that managers oversee certain sections of the restaurant or are in charge at specific times. The roles of various managers might include the following:

- Personnel managers supervise effective employment orientation, training, and management of employees.
- Purchasing managers maintain profitability of units by controlling costs, authorizing expenditures, and reviewing results.
- Operations managers enforce consistent company standards, systems, and procedures.
- Marketing and promotions managers implement store marketing concepts, programs, and advertising campaigns.
- Finance managers monitor performance, prepare budgets, and develop sales forecasts.

The various titles of those who oversee sections of the restaurant include:

| | |
|---|---|
| Kitchen manager | District manager |
| Dining room manager | Unit manager |
| Night manager | Assistant unit manager |
| Regional manager | |

Depending on the size and business hours of a restaurant, managers may be assisted by one or more assistant managers. In large establishments as well as many others that offer fine dining, the management team consists of a general manager, one or more assistant managers, and an executive chef. The executive chef is responsible for the operation of the kitchen, while the assistant managers oversee service in the dining room and other areas of the operation. However, in smaller establishments, the executive chef may also be the general manager and sometimes the owner.

Obviously, managers of small operations perform more varied tasks, while managers in larger establishments have more specialized responsibilities.

## Nature of Management Work

The efficient and profitable operation of restaurants requires that managers select and appropriately price interesting menu items; make efficient use of food, beverages, and other supplies; achieve consistent quality in food preparation and service; recruit and train adequate numbers of workers; and painstakingly attend to the various administrative aspects of the business.

Managers or executive chefs select menu items, taking into account the likely number of customers, the past popularity of various dishes, and considerations such as leftover food that should not be wasted. They also address issues such as the need for variety on the menu and the availability of foods due to seasonal and other factors.

Managers analyze the recipes of the dishes to determine food, labor, and overhead costs and assign prices to the menu items. Menus must be developed far enough in advance to receive needed supplies in time.

On a daily basis, managers estimate food consumption, place orders with suppliers, and schedule the delivery of fresh food and beverages. They receive and check the contents of deliveries, evaluating the quality of meats, poultry, fish, fruits, vegetables, and baked goods.

Managers meet and talk with sales representatives of restaurant suppliers to place orders to replenish stocks of tableware, linens, paper, cleaning supplies, cooking utensils, and furniture and fixtures. They also arrange for equipment repairs.

Managers recruit, interview, hire, and, when necessary, discharge workers. They familiarize newly hired workers with the establishment's policies and practices and oversee their training. Managers schedule the work hours of employees, ensuring that there are adequate numbers of workers present during busy periods but not too many during slow periods.

Managers supervise the preparation of food in the kitchen and the serving of meals in the dining room. They oversee food preparation and cooking, checking the quality of the food and the sizes of portions to ensure that dishes are prepared and garnished correctly and in a timely manner.

If customers complain about service or food quality, it is the manager's job to investigate and resolve the issue. Often, this will mean offering the customer a complimentary drink or dessert along with a sincere apology. People skills are essential during these times and will make the difference between good and bad word of mouth advertising.

Managers direct the cleaning of the kitchen and dining areas and the washing of tableware, kitchen utensils, and equipment to maintain company and government sanitation standards. Managers monitor workers and observe patrons on a continual basis to make sure that the restaurant complies with health and safety standards as well as local liquor regulations. During busy periods, managers often have to roll up their sleeves and help with the cooking, cleaning of tables, or other tasks.

Managers also have a variety of administrative responsibilities. In larger establishments, much of this work is done by a bookkeeper, but in others, managers are responsible for keeping accurate records of the hours and wages of employees, preparing the payroll, and doing paperwork to comply with licensing laws and reporting requirements of tax, wage and hour, unemployment compensation, and Social Security laws. They also must maintain records of the costs of supplies and equipment purchased and ensure that accounts with suppliers are paid on a regular basis.

In addition, managers record the number, type, and cost of items sold to weed out dishes that are unpopular or less profitable. The vast majority of managers now use computers to help ease the burden of paperwork.

At the end of each day or sometimes each shift, managers must tally the cash and credit card receipts and balance them against the records of sales. They are responsible for depositing the day's income at the bank or securing it in a safe place. Managers also are responsible for locking the doors and making sure that all ovens, grills, and lights are off and all alarm systems are switched on.

## Working Conditions

Managers are the first to arrive and the last to leave at night. Because evenings and weekends are popular dining periods, night and weekend work is common. Many restaurant managers work sixty hours or more each week. Managers in institutional food-service facilities work more conventional hours because factory and office cafeterias are open only on weekdays for breakfast and lunch.

Restaurant managers sometimes experience the pressures of coordinating a wide range of functions. The job can be hectic during peak dining hours, and dealing with irate customers or uncooperative employees can be particularly stressful. However, the working conditions are usually clean, well lighted, and air-conditioned.

## Employment

Recent statistics show that there are approximately 470,000 restaurant managers. Most work in eating and drinking establishments, but small numbers also work in educational institutions; hospitals, nursing, and personal care facilities; department stores; and civic, social, and fraternal organizations.

Most managers are salaried, but about one-third of managers are self-employed. Jobs are located throughout the country but are most plentiful in large cities and tourist areas.

## Training

The promotion of experienced food and beverage preparation and service workers fills some restaurant management positions. Waiters, waitresses, chefs, and fast-food workers who have demonstrated their potential for handling increased responsibilities sometimes advance to assistant manager or management-trainee jobs if openings occur.

Just as executive chefs need extensive experience working as a chef, general managers need experience working as an assistant. However, most food-service management companies and national or regional chains also recruit management trainees from among the graduates of two-year and four-year college programs.

Food-service and restaurant chains prefer to hire persons with degrees in restaurant and institutional food-service management, but they often hire graduates who have degrees in other fields and who have demonstrated interest and aptitude.

A bachelor's degree in restaurant and food-service management provides a particularly strong preparation for a career in this occupation. A number of colleges and universities offer four-year programs in restaurant and hotel management or in institutional food-service management.

For persons who do not want to pursue a four-year degree, a good alternative background is provided by the more than eight hundred community and junior colleges, technical institutes, and other institutions that offer programs in these fields leading to an associate degree or other formal award below the baccalaureate.

Both two-year and four-year programs provide instruction in subjects such as accounting, business law and management, computer science, food planning and preparation, and nutrition. In some instances, courses are offered online. Some programs combine classroom and laboratory study with internships that provide on-the-job experience.

In addition, many educational institutions offer culinary programs that provide food preparation training, which can lead to a career as a cook or chef and provide a foundation for advancement to an executive chef position.

## Other Qualifications

Perhaps as in no other industry, the emphasis for restaurant employees is on personal qualities. The right personality is a crucial factor. Restaurant managers must genuinely like and understand people. To the restaurant staff, they must be fair and respected for their leadership. To customers, they must appear hardworking, sympathetic, and capable of dealing with almost any situation or demand, often under pressure.

Because restaurant management can be so demanding, good health and stamina are important attributes for a manager to have. Self-discipline, initiative, and leadership ability are essential. Managers must be able to make decisions, solve problems, and concentrate on details. Good communication skills are necessary to deal with customers and suppliers as well as to direct subordinates. A neat and clean appearance is required, and a sense of humor is an asset.

Most companies offer extensive management-trainee programs. Through a combination of classroom and on-the-job training, trainees receive instruction and gain work experience in all aspects of restaurant operation including food preparation, sanitation, security, company policies and procedures, personnel management, record keeping, and preparation of reports. Usually after six months or a year, trainees receive their first permanent assignment as an assistant manager.

## Advancement

Willingness to relocate often is essential for advancement to positions with greater responsibility. Managers advance to larger establishments or regional management positions with restaurant chains. Some managers eventually open their own restaurants. Others are able to transfer to hotel management positions because their experience is a good background for food and beverage manager jobs at hotels and resorts.

## Job Outlook

Employment of restaurant managers is expected to increase about as fast as the average for all occupations through 2010. In addition to growth in demand for these managers, the need to replace managers who transfer to other occupations or stop working for a variety of reasons will create many new jobs. Opportunities are expected to be best for persons with bachelor's or associate degrees in restaurant institutional food-service management.

Employment will increase with growth in the number of eating and drinking establishments. Population growth, rising personal incomes, increased leisure time, and more two-income families are factors that will continue to add to the number of meals consumed outside the home.

Rather than be independently owned or operated, new restaurants are increasingly affiliated with national chains. As this trend continues, fewer owners will manage restaurants and more restaurant managers will be employed to do so. Growth in the number of elderly people is expected to create rapid growth of food-service management positions in nursing homes, residential-care facilities, and other health-care institutions.

## Earnings

According to the type and size of establishment, earnings of restaurant and food-service managers vary greatly. Median annual earnings of food-service managers are $31,720. However, managers of the largest restaurants and institutional food-service facilities often have annual salaries in excess of $53,000.

According to a survey conducted by the National Restaurant Association, the median base salary for a unit manager is $35,132 and for an assistant unit manager, $28,000. District managers receive a median base salary of $53,262 and an annual bonus of $10,000. Regional managers receive a median base salary of $62,500 and a median annual bonus of $15,000. Kitchen managers receive a median base salary of $29,000. The median base salary for a manager trainee is $25,080.

Among chef positions, the median base salary for the executive chef is $48,000, for a sous chef $30,000, and for a pastry chef $30,000.

Most restaurant and food-service managers receive free meals, sick leave, health and accident insurance, one to three weeks of paid vacation a year, and the opportunity for additional training depending on length of service.

## Food and Beverage Directors

Food and beverage directors are responsible for the overall operation and coordination of all food and beverage departments in hotels, motels, and some fine restaurants that have large staffs. As we've seen, many food-service jobs overlap one another. The smaller the operation, the more hats each employee wears; the larger the establishment, the more specialized the jobs become. But food and beverage directors oversee all of these specialized jobs.

### Nature of the Job

Food and beverage directors oversee the work of the purchasing, kitchen, and dining room staffs. They must possess a thorough knowledge of all the jobs the workers on these staffs perform because they are responsible for selecting, training, and motivating each staff member.

The purchasing staff buys food for the chef and kitchen staff to prepare. The dining room staff serves the guests. A major responsibility of food and beverage directors is to coordinate the efforts of the three staffs from start to finish, and they must do it in a way that maintains and improves productivity, food quality, service, creativity, and merchandising in order to increase volume, sales, and profits.

To provide the best possible service to guests, food and beverage directors must keep other operating departments informed concerning the activities of the food and beverage department. They must ensure that the decisions made correspond to those of the general manager and the approved policies of the establishment. If necessary, food and beverage directors recommend changes or innovations in policy, procedure, or equipment to management.

Food and beverage directors schedule the times of operation of all restaurants and bars to achieve the most profitable result. They establish purchasing and receiving procedures and ensure that all the supplies ordered are received in the quantities requested, as well as in proper condition.

Food and beverage directors assess and analyze competitors; they review prices, sources of supply, food and beverage trends, and inventories. They also hire and discharge workers.

### Working Conditions

Because food and beverage directors are involved in administrative work, they usually have their own private offices. However, their responsibilities take them to all parts of the restaurant, and they are on their feet a good part of the day. Although they are usually scheduled to work about forty hours a week, many times they must work more than that. Their hours may be irregular because they supervise workers in various shifts. They sometimes experience the pressures of coordinating a wide range of functions. In hotels, conventions and large groups of tourists can cause additional stress for food and beverage directors.

## Employment

Because each hotel has only one food and beverage director, the competition can be keen. Thus, possessing some college education or other training will put you ahead of applicants without formal education. Jobs are located throughout the country but are most plentiful in large cities and tourist areas.

## Training

Postsecondary training in hotel or restaurant management is preferred for most food and beverage director positions, although a college liberal arts degree may be sufficient when coupled with related hotel experience. In the past, most food and beverage directors were promoted from the ranks of lower positions within the establishment. Some persons can still become food and beverage directors without the benefit of education beyond high school, but this is becoming more and more difficult.

Specialized hotel experience is an asset to all persons seeking food and beverage management careers. In many hotel chains, specialized hotel or restaurant training is preferred or even required. Because a hotel's restaurant and cocktail lounge are often of great importance to the success of the entire establishment, restaurant management training or experience is an acceptable background for entering hotel management.

A bachelor's degree in hospitality and restaurant administration provides particularly strong preparation for a career as a food and beverage director. Today numerous colleges and universities offer four-year programs in hotel management. In addition, more than a thousand community and junior colleges, technical institutes, vocational and trade schools, culinary schools, and other academic institutions also have programs leading to an associate degree or other formal recognition in hospitality or restaurant management. (See Appendixes A and B.) Graduates of hospitality or restaurant management programs are able to start as trainee assistant managers or at least advance to such positions more quickly.

## Other Qualifications

Food and beverage directors must be able to get along with all kinds of people, even in the most stressful situations. They need initiative, self-discipline, and the ability to organize and direct the work of others. They must have the ability to solve problems and concentrate on details. Some hotels insist that food and beverage directors speak one or two languages in addition to English.

## Advancement

Most hotels promote employees who have proven their ability. Newly built hotels, particularly those without well-established, on-the-job training programs, often prefer experienced personnel for managerial positions. Large hotels and motel chains may offer managers better opportunities for advancement than small, independently owned establishments, but frequent relocation is often necessary. Large chains also can offer more extensive career ladder opportunities to food and beverage directors, who may be given the chance to transfer to another hotel or motel in the chain or to the central office if an opening occurs.

## *Job Outlook*

Employment of food and beverage directors is expected to increase about as fast as the average for all occupations through 2010. Most openings are expected to occur as experienced food and beverage directors transfer, retire, or stop working. Applicants with a bachelor's or associate degree in restaurant and institutional food-service management should have the best job opportunities.

## *Earnings*

According to a National Restaurant Association survey, food and beverage directors average an estimated $44,200 a year. In some establishments, food and beverage directors may earn bonuses ranging up to 20 percent of their base salary. They and their families also may be eligible for lodging, meals, parking, laundry, and other services.

**5**

# CERTIFIED MASTER CHEF: THE HIGHEST HONOR IN THE INDUSTRY

THERE ARE FIFTY-EIGHT certified master chefs (CMCs) in the United States. This designation, acknowledged worldwide, represents the highest recognition a professional chef can attain. Europe, which has been implementing the master certification program for more than half a century, has thousands of certified master chefs. But the title and the distinction is a new one in the United States. It was offered for the first time in 1981.

The fifty-eight CMCs are highly trained individuals who are deeply dedicated to their profession.

## The Master Chef Certification Program

Master chef certification (MCC) results from the most rigorous testing a professional chef can encounter. Ferdinand Metz, president of the Culinary Institute of America in Hyde Park, New York, from 1980 to 2001, was the driving force behind developing the MCC program.

"When I was charged with the task of developing an MCC program, I went to very logical sources—primarily my brother and my father, who are both certified master chefs in Europe. From them, my training in Europe, and my travels, I was able to compile a comprehensive program," he says.

"The program in the United States had to be more stringent and more comprehensive than its foreign counterparts, because America is comprised of a combination of almost every nation; whereas in Europe most chefs focus on classical cuisine with a bit of regional cooking. It was my intention to establish a program that would have integrity and would be mutually recognized under the reciprocal arrangement with any nation in Europe. That was achieved."

Each candidate for master chef certification is a certified executive chef with many years of experience in the world of food. Candidates for MCC enroll in the American Culinary Federation's intensive ten-day program. The test is held annually—provided there is a minimum of six registered candidates—at two approved test sites: the Culinary Institute of America in New York, and Greystone, the CIA's West Coast campus in Napa Valley, California. Candidates must complete the required course load, which includes the following topics:

- Food safety and sanitation
- Nutrition
- Hospitality supervision
- American cuisine
- International cuisine

- Classical cuisine
- Bakery/pastry/patisserie
- Dietary cooking/nutrition
- Tableside cooking
- Cold buffet preparation
- Menu development
- Managerial development
- Beverage control and service

Once the course load is completed, all candidates are required to pass theoretical and practical examinations.

Chefs spend a great deal of time studying for these examinations. Some CMCs have reported spending six months in intensive preparation, studying sixteen hours a day. In addition to their time, chefs invest from $4,000 to $6,000 in tuition, fees, travel, materials, and living expenses.

## Passing the Exam

After a lifetime of preparation and months of intensive study, the chefs undergo examinations that begin at 7:00 A.M. and end at 9:00 P.M. Candidates are required to perform under the constant, watchful eye of judges and students. Obviously, chefs must be in top mental and physical shape to begin a testing program of this intensity.

Food must be prepared at the exact time specified—not five minutes before or five minutes after. This pressure causes burnout for some candidates, who depart before the program's completion. The success rate has been a discouragingly low 45 percent. However, chefs who have successfully completed the program support its structure. One CMC explained it this way: "The testing has to be as tough and intensive as it is because a chef must work well under pressure. If you can't, then you're not a master."

## Rewards of Becoming a CMC

One might wonder why successful, well-respected professionals would subject themselves to this kind of rigorous testing. The certified master chefs said the challenge of the program was a very appealing factor. But the motivating factor is that they want to advance the profession as well as set an example for student chefs and peers.

Aside from the great honor attached to being classified as the best, master chef certification also includes privileges, rewards, and responsibilities. The privileges include being recognized as a top professional in the culinary field, assuming a professional leadership role, and upgrading culinary standards. More tangible rewards include job offers, raises, promotions, and publicity. Master chef certification brings status to the CMC's establishment and provides inspiration to others wishing to attain the same distinction.

There are responsibilities that come with the title. Once granted master chef certification, chefs administer future examinations to guarantee quality control. Other responsibilities include:

- Maintaining and upgrading the high standards of the culinary arts
- Representing the profession outside the industry
- Supporting the American Culinary Foundation (ACF) by lecturing, teaching ACF apprentices, and serving as judges for national and international competitions

After becoming a CMC and receiving the highest honor the profession can bestow, certified master chefs still have a challenge: it is to live up to their reputations, to continue learning, and to pass their knowledge on to other chefs.

## How the CMC Program Benefits the Restaurant Industry

Certified Master Chef Ferdinand Metz summed up the program's value to the restaurant industry in this way: "When I came to this country in 1962, anybody could put on a white hat and claim to be a chef. No one could dispute it. Food service at that time was in sad, sad shape. Today it has improved tremendously. Almost 100 percent of the thousands of students CIA graduates every year have master chef certification as their ultimate goal. When they achieve this goal, it will tell them something about themselves, and it will also tell the outside world about them. Becoming a CMC is a culmination of many years of experience, which add up to quality, expertise, professionalism, and recognition.

"The master chef certification program is still in its infancy in the United States. Relatively few people outside of the industry have ever heard of it. Once it becomes more widely known—and it will be—the public will render the title of Certified Master Chef its just respect and admiration. When that happens, the entire food-service industry will benefit."

# 6

## Top Executives in the Restaurant Industry

THE RESTAURANT INDUSTRY is distinct in that the owner of a single-unit, twenty-seat diner, who may have to wash dishes and sweep the floor, is also the establishment's chief executive officer. This owner would be the chairperson of the board—if there were a board of directors—and president, even though there may be only one employee. As the top executive, a single-unit owner is responsible for making the decisions on how to run the business. He or she owns the establishment, and that says it all.

Although one-unit owners may have a common bond with the owners of very large, international chains such as McDonald's or Burger King, their average workdays and their average salaries are very different.

In this chapter, the focus is on those restaurant establishments large enough to require top executives to oversee the managers. These individuals have reached the top of the management ladder and are sometimes called general managers or executive vice presidents.

General managers and executive vice presidents are responsible for planning, organizing, directing, controlling, and coordinating the operations of an organization and its major departments or programs. The members of the board of directors and supervisory managers also are involved in these activities.

Individual departments that general managers and executive vice presidents oversee include the following:

- Operations
- Finance
- Marketing
- Advertising
- Human relations
- Distribution/purchasing
- Recruitment
- Training

## Nature of the Work

The fundamental objective of any business venture, including all types of restaurant establishments, is to maintain efficiency and profitability in the face of accelerating technological complexity and acute and ever-increasing competition.

In collaboration with other top executives, usually executive vice presidents and the board of directors, the chief executive officer establishes the general goals and policies of a large restaurant corporation. Often busy chief executive officers meet with top executives of similar restaurant establishments to discuss matters affecting the industry. Although the chief executive officer retains ultimate authority and responsibility, the chief operating officer may be delegated the authority to oversee executive vice presidents, who direct the activities of various departments and are responsible for carrying out the organization's goals.

The responsibilities of executive vice presidents depend greatly upon the size of the restaurant establishment. In large corporations, their duties may be highly specialized. For example, they may oversee the activities of general managers of marketing, sales promotion, purchasing, finance, personnel, training, administrative service, property management, or legal services. In smaller establishments, an executive vice president might be responsible for a number of these departments.

General managers, in turn, direct their individual department's activities within the framework of the organization's overall plan. With the help of supervisory managers and their staffs, general managers strive to achieve the department's goals as rapidly and economically as possible.

## Working Conditions

It is not unusual for top executives to be provided with spacious, lavish offices, and many enjoy numerous benefits. General managers are provided with comfortable offices close to the departments they direct and to the executive vice presidents to whom they report. Long hours, including evenings and weekends, are the rule, and business discussions might occupy most of their time during social engagements.

Substantial travel is often required. General managers may have to travel between national, regional, and local offices. Executive vice presidents may travel to meet with their counterparts in other corporations in the country, or even overseas. Meetings and conferences sponsored by industries and associations occur regularly and provide invaluable opportunities to meet with peers and keep abreast of technological and other developments. A prime example of this is the National Restaurant Association's annual show, held in the spring.

In large corporations, job transfers between the parent company and its local offices or subsidiaries both here or abroad are common.

General managers and top executives of restaurant operations very often work under intense pressure to attain their goals. Sometimes they find themselves in situations over which they have limited influence, for example, when meeting with government officials, private interest groups, or competitors.

## Employment

According to the latest figures available, general managers and top executives hold about three million jobs, but not all in the restaurant industry. Although these positions are found in every industry, employment is more concentrated in the largest industries such as the restaurant business.

## Training

The educational background of managers and top executives varies as widely as the nature of their diverse responsibilities. Most general managers and top executives have a bachelor's degree in liberal arts or business administration. Their academic major is often related to the departments they direct—for example, accounting for a general manager of finance or computer science for a general manager of data processing. Graduate and professional degrees are common. Many managers in administrative, marketing, financial, and manufacturing activities have a master's degree in business administration.

Managers in highly technical manufacturing and research activities, such as food technology, often have a master's or doctoral degree in an engineering or scientific discipline. A law degree is necessary for general managers of corporate legal departments.

In the restaurant industry, as well as in retail trade, competent individuals without a college degree may become general managers; however, for most general managers, experience is still the primary qualification.

Most general management and top executive positions are filled by promoting experienced lower-level managers who display the leadership, self-confidence, motivation, decisiveness, and flexibility required by these demanding positions. In small firms, where the number of positions is limited, advancement to a higher management position may come slowly. In large firms, promotions may occur more quickly. Those who wish to accelerate the advancement process should take advantage of company training programs to broaden their knowledge of company policy and operations.

For example, attendance at seminars sponsored by the National Restaurant Association and held throughout the country can familiarize managers with the latest developments in management techniques. Participation in these conferences and seminars can expand one's knowledge of national and international issues influencing the restaurant industry.

Persons interested in becoming general managers and top executives must possess well-developed personal skills. A highly analytical mind able to quickly assess large amounts of information and data is very important, as is the ability to consider and evaluate the interrelationships of numerous factors and to select the best course of action. In the absence of sufficient information, sound intuitive managerial judgment is crucial to reaching favorable decisions. General managers and top executives also must be able to communicate clearly and persuasively, both orally and in writing.

General managers may advance to a top executive position, such as executive or administrative vice president, in their own establishment or to a corresponding general management position in a larger establishment. Similarly, top-level managers may advance to peak corporate positions such as chief operating officer and finally chief executive officer. Chief executive officers, upon retirement, may become members of the board of directors of one or more firms. Some general managers and top executives with sufficient capital establish their own restaurant businesses.

## Job Outlook

Employment of general managers and top executives is expected to increase about as fast as the average for all occupations through 2010 as businesses grow in number, size, and complexity. However, much-faster-than-average employment growth is projected in the hotel, restaurant, and travel industries as personal income and leisure time increase. In addition to openings arising from increased demand for these managers and executives, many job openings will occur each year to replace those who transfer to better-paying positions, start their own businesses, or retire.

However, the ample supply of competent and experienced lower-level managers seeking top management positions should result in substantial job competition. Outstanding individuals whose accomplishments reflect leadership qualities and the ability to improve the efficiency or competitive position of the organization will have the best employment opportunities.

# Earnings

Recent figures indicate that the estimated median annual salary of general managers and top executives is approximately $61,200. Their salaries range from $38,710 to $101,340. Salary levels vary substantially depending upon the level of managerial responsibility, length of service, and the type, size, and location of the firm.

Most salaried general managers and top executives in the restaurant industry receive additional compensation in the form of bonuses, stock awards, and cash-equivalent fringe benefits such as company-paid insurance premiums, use of company cars, and paid country club or health club memberships.

Chief executive officers of large corporations are the most highly paid top-level managers. One survey of top publicly held corporations revealed that more than a hundred chief executive officers received base salaries of $1 million or more, with additional compensation such as fringe benefits and company stock equaling, on average, nearly half of their base salary. Other surveys of executive salaries reveal the importance of the size of the corporation. A top-level manager in a very large corporation can earn ten times as much as a counterpart in a small firm.

Salaries also vary substantially by industry and geographic location. For example, salaries in large metropolitan areas such as New York City are normally higher than those in small cities and towns.

# 7

---

# BEHIND-THE-SCENE WORKERS

THIS CHAPTER FOCUSES on positions that have recently become more and more important to the restaurant industry. These positions include dietitians, menu planners, and food scientists-technologists. Often these individuals work in offices or laboratories away from the restaurant operation, but their influence can be found in all segments of the restaurant industry, from the chefs who prepare the food to the customers enjoying it.

## Dietitians and Nutritionists

Dietitians, sometimes called nutritionists, are professionals trained in applying the principles of nutrition to food selection and meal preparation.

In today's society, there is a growing concern for physical fitness and healthful eating habits. Restaurant operators are aware of this trend, and many are taking steps to alter their menus accordingly.

An increasing number of restaurant operators are hiring or, at least, consulting with dietitians and nutritionists when planning their food offerings.

Dietitians and nutritionists perform the following services:

- Counsel individuals and groups in the basics of sound nutrition to promote good health
- Set up and supervise food-service systems for institutions such as hospitals, prisons, schools, and large restaurant chains
- Promote sound eating habits through education and research
- Analyze the nutritional content of food for labeling purposes or marketing efforts

In addition to restaurants, dietitians may run the food-service departments of small hospitals. In this capacity, dietitians are responsible for establishing long-term nutritional-care programs and a system of close monitoring of individual patients. When necessary, they must be able to prepare custom-mixed, high-nutrition formulas for patients who require tube or intravenous feedings. Administrative dietitians are responsible for large-scale meal planning and preparation in places such as hospitals, company cafeterias, prisons, schools, and colleges and universities.

Dietitians and nutritionists perform the following tasks:

- Supervise the planning, preparation, and serving of meals
- Select, train, and direct food-service supervisors and workers
- Budget for and purchase food, equipment, and supplies
- Enforce sanitary and safety regulations
- Prepare records and reports

Increasingly, dietitians use computer programs to plan meals that satisfy nutritional requirements and are economical at the same time. Dietitians who are directors of dietetic departments also decide on departmental policy, coordinate dietetic services with the activities of other departments, and develop and maintain the dietetic department budget, which in large organizations may amount to millions of dollars annually.

Research dietitians use established research methods and analytical techniques to conduct studies in areas that range from basic science to practical applications. Research dietitians may examine changes in the way the body uses food over the course of a lifetime, for example, or study the interaction of drugs and diet. They may investigate nutritional needs of persons with particular diseases, behavior modification as it relates to diet and nutrition, or applied topics such as food-service systems and equipment.

Often research dietitians are called on to make their findings known to the restaurant industry by preparing research papers and oral presentations.

## Working Conditions

Most dietitians work forty hours a week. Those who are employed in hospitals sometimes work on weekends, while those in commercial food services tend to have irregular hours.

Dietitians and nutritionists spend much of their time in clean, well-lighted, and well-ventilated areas such as research laboratories, classrooms, or offices near food preparation areas. However, they may spend time in kitchens and serving areas that are often hot and steamy and where some light lifting may be required. Dietitians and nutritionists may be on their feet for most of the workday. Those who are involved in consulting spend a significant amount of time traveling.

## Employment

Recent statistics show that dietitians and nutritionists hold about 49,000 jobs. Hospitals and nursing homes are a major source of employment for dietitians and nutritionists, accounting for just over half of all jobs in this field. Firms that provide food services for hospital patients on a contract basis employ a small but growing number of dietitians and nutritionists.

Local government programs and schools, colleges, and universities provide about 10 percent of dietitian jobs. Other jobs for dietitians and nutritionists are found in prison systems, hotel and restaurant chains, school systems, and companies that provide food service for their employees.

Many dietitians and nutritionists work as consultants, either full-time or part-time. In addition to serving on the staff of a hospital, for example, a dietitian may be a consultant for another health-care facility. Some dietitians are self-employed, working as consultants to facilities such as hospitals and nursing homes, or providing dietary counseling to individual clients.

## Training

The basic requirement for this field is a bachelor's degree with a major in dietetics, foods and nutrition, or institution management. This degree can be earned in about 234 colleges and universities, usually in departments of home economics or food and nutrition sciences. In addition to basic educational requirements, required college courses include foods, nutrition, institution management, chemistry, biochemistry, biology, microbiology, and physiology. Other important courses are business, mathematics, statistics, computer science, psychology, sociology, and economics.

Of the forty-one states that have laws governing dietetics, twenty-seven require licensure, thirteen require certification, and one requires registration. The Commission on Dietetic Registration of the American Dietetic Association (ADA) awards the Registered Dietitian credential to those who pass a certification exam after completing their academic education and supervised experience.

As of 2001, there were 234 ADA-approved bachelor's degree programs. Supervised practice experience can be acquired in two ways: First, there are fifty-one ADA-accredited coordinated programs that combine academic and supervised practice experience in a four-year program. The second option requires completion of nine hundred hours of supervised practice experience, in one of the 258 ADA-accredited internships. Internships and preprofessional practice programs may be full-time programs lasting six to twelve months or part-time programs lasting two years. Students interested in research, advanced clinical positions, or public health should get a graduate degree.

## Other Qualifications

Persons who are planning to become dietitians or nutritionists should have organizational and administrative ability as well as scientific aptitude. They also should be able to work well with people.

Among the courses recommended for high school students interested in a career as a dietitian are home economics, business, biology, health, mathematics, communications, and chemistry.

Computer courses are valuable because dietitians and nutritionists use computers for planning meals, keeping inventory, and analyzing the nutritional content of proposed diets.

## Advancement

Experienced dietitians and nutritionists may advance to assistant or associate director or director of a dietetic department. Advancement to higher-level positions in teaching and research requires graduate education; public health nutritionists usually must earn a graduate degree. Graduate study in institutional or business administration is valuable for those interested in administrative dietetics.

Clinical specialization offers another path to career advancement. Specialty areas for clinical dietitians include kidney disease, diabetes, cancer, heart disease, pediatrics, and gerontology.

## Job Outlook

Employment of dietitians and nutritionists is expected to grow about as fast as the average for all occupations through 2010 due to increased emphasis on disease prevention by improved health habits. A growing and aging population will increase the need for individual and group meals in nursing homes, schools, hospitals, retirement and life-care communities, and social service programs of various kinds. However, most job openings will result from the need to replace experienced workers who stop working or change occupations. A number of experienced dietitians and nutritionists are moving into management positions in private industry, including food-service establishments.

The factors that underlie anticipated rapid expansion of the health services industry—population growth and aging, emphasis on health education, and promotion of prudent lifestyles and eating habits, as well as widespread ability to pay for care through public and private health insurance—will increase the demand for dietitians and nutritionists.

Employment of dietitians in hospitals is expected to grow slowly because of anticipated slow growth in the number of inpatients and as hospitals contract out food-service operations. On the other hand, faster than average growth in employment is expected in nursing homes as the number of very old people rises sharply, in contract providers of food services, in residential-care facilities, in offices and clinics of physicians, and in other social services.

Employment growth for dietitians and nutritionists may be somewhat constrained by the substitutability of other workers such as nurses, health educators, food-service managers, and dietetic technicians. Growth also would be faster except for limitations on insurance reimbursement for dietetic services.

Opportunities will be best for individuals with experience and for those willing to relocate to areas of greatest demand.

## Earnings

According to the most recent figures available, median annual earnings of dietitians and nutritionists are $38,450. Entry-level salaries of dietitians average $23,680 a year, and maximum salaries average about $54,940. According to the American Dietetic Association, median annual income for registered dietitians in food and nutrition management is approximately $48,370. Salaries vary by years in practice, educational level, region, and size of community.

Dietitians and nutritionists usually receive benefits such as paid vacations, sick leave, holidays, health insurance, and retirement benefits.

# Menu Planners

The menu planner's work is similar to the work of dietitians and nutritionists; however, it is not quite so technical and it doesn't require the same amount of education.

## Nature of the Work

Menu planners do exactly what their title implies: they decide what dishes are to be offered to restaurant or institutional patrons. Menu planners are charged with planning menus that are nutritionally balanced, pleasing to the eye, and possible to prepare in large quantities. Menu planners must keep many factors in mind while doing their job, specifically taste, color, nutrition, and cost.

Because restaurant patrons are constantly seeking the new and exciting side of food, menu planners are continually revising menus, developing new recipes, and introducing new dishes to please the customers. A constant challenge for menu planners in large institutional cafeterias is to put variety into the menus. They meet this challenge by ordering unusual ingredients and discovering new recipes.

Menu planners work with cooks, chefs, and other dining room and kitchen workers to ask advice, make suggestions, and solve technical problems. At times, the executive chef supervises their work.

Menu planners who work in national chain restaurants try to standardize recipes so that a bowl of onion soup in San Francisco tastes the same as one in Minneapolis. Menu planners who are employed by franchise companies also are concerned with trying to make food produced in very large quantities look and taste as though it was individually prepared.

Menu planners can advance to food and beverage managers, catering managers, or directors of all dining facilities. Advancement opportunities are usually greatest in large hotels, restaurants, and institutions.

## Working Conditions

Generally, menu planners enjoy very pleasant working conditions. They spend most of their time sitting at a desk in clean, well-lit offices conveniently located near the kitchen. Their jobs are much less stressful than those of other restaurant employees because they work behind the scene and are not subject to demands of evening, holiday, or weekend crowds.

Menu planners usually work in large restaurants, hotels, hospitals, prisons, airlines, schools and universities, cafeterias, and other large dining facilities.

## Training

Often individual college course work in dietetics or nutrition is enough to qualify for the position of menu planner. However, a bachelor's degree in one of these fields is sometimes required and never wasted. Would-be menu planners can find excellent courses—including food technology, recipe development, and quantity food production, for example—at vocational schools. Some chain restaurants and large hotels offer on-the-job training as well.

Menu planners must have the ability to imagine how food will look on a customer's plate. A good sense of taste and smell is also necessary. As with any job in the restaurant industry, a menu planner must work well with people.

## *Job Outlook*

Employment of menu planners is expected to grow faster than the average for all occupations through 2010 to meet the expanding need for such services. Most job openings will result from the need to replace experienced workers who stop working or change occupations. A number of experienced menu planners move into management positions. Menu planners who have a strong background in dietetics may want to work in the food production industry. Opportunities will be best for individuals with experience and for those willing to relocate to areas of greatest demand.

## *Earnings*

The average salary for menu planners trained in vocational schools is about $21,000 to $25,000 a year. Salaries may vary by region. Menu planners usually receive benefits such as free meals, paid vacations, sick leave, holidays, health insurance, and pension plans.

# Food Scientists-Technologists

As our world becomes more and more sophisticated, new and more technical jobs are created. For example, to meet the food requirements of men and women in today's changing environment, food scientists-technologists are needed.

According to experts at the Institute of Food Technologists in Chicago, the need for food research is creating a steady demand for persons trained as food scientists-technologists. According to Professor William Marion, head of the Food Technology Department at Iowa State University, the field is becoming more precisely defined in light of new research findings: "In the past, the food scientist-technologist was simply called a food technologist," he said. "Within that broad heading, he or she performed a number of scientific and technical tasks. Today, this person is now called a food scientist-technologist."

## Nature of the Work

A food scientist-technologist, depending on the company or organization he or she is working for, may function as a scientist or technologist or both. But Marion maintains that it is important to draw the line between the two sets of responsibilities. "Generally speaking, the food scientist is concerned with the fundamental properties of food, taking into effect color, nutritive value, and caloric content. If you were working as a technologist, you would be involved with product development, processing, and quality control."

## Working Conditions

Approximately one-third of all food scientists-technologists work in research and development, while others work in quality assurance laboratories in production or processing areas of food plants. A small number teach or do basic research in colleges and universities. Others hold sales and management positions.

Food scientists-technologists search for ways to retain the characteristics and nutritive value of foods during processing and storage. They also supervise chemical and microbiological tests to see that products meet industry and government requirements. For example, processed foods must be tested for sugar, starch, protein, fat, vitamin, and mineral content.

Food scientists-technologists work in quality control laboratories, where they study raw ingredients for freshness, maturity, and suitability for processing. They regularly inspect processing-line operations to ensure conformance with government and industry standards. Food scientists-technologists must be sure that after processing, various enzymes are inactive and bacterial levels are low enough so that food will not spoil or present a safety hazard.

Food scientists-technologists who work in processing plants have a number of different responsibilities, which include the following:

- Preparing production specifications
- Scheduling processing operations
- Maintaining proper temperature and humidity in storage areas
- Supervising sanitation operations, including the proper disposal of wastes
- Advising management concerning the purchase of equipment and supplies to increase efficiency

## Employment and Training

Recent statistics indicate that agricultural and food scientists hold about seventeen thousand jobs. Several thousand persons also hold agricultural science faculty positions in colleges and universities.

Food scientists-technologists should have a bachelor's degree in food technology. There are about forty universities around the country offering programs in food technology. For students who want to break into the industry gradually, junior and community colleges offer associate certificates in the food processing area.

## *Earnings*

Salaries within the food scientist-technologist field vary with educational background and type of organization. Large companies generally pay better than government agencies and universities. The median annual earnings of food scientists are approximately $52,160. The lowest 10 percent earns less than $31,910, and the highest 10 percent earns more than $83,740. Food scientists-technologists may start out as junior food chemists in the research and development lab. Once they gain experience, it is possible to move into management positions.

## *Job Outlook*

Opportunities for food scientists-technologists are expected to grow more slowly than the average for all occupations through 2010. The need to replace food scientists who retire or otherwise leave the occupation permanently will account for many more job openings than will projected growth, particularly in academia.

However, an expanding population and an increasing public focus on diet, health, and food safety will result in job opportunities for food scientists and technologists. Graduates with advanced degrees will be in the best position to enter jobs as food scientists and technologists.

# 8

# Running Your Own Restaurant

It's possible for you to own and operate your own restaurant. You can be the boss, make the decisions, and take responsibility for failure or success. But before considering the idea, you must realize that owning a restaurant is extremely hard work. The venture will consume all of your time—including evenings, weekends, and holidays—and, at least in the beginning, it will be very expensive.

If you have seriously considered these facts, believe in the reality of them, realize there is absolutely no guarantee of success, and still want to own and operate your own restaurant, congratulations. You may have made a very rewarding and lucrative decision. Here are some things you should do to avoid common downfalls and help ensure success.

## Gain Restaurant Experience Elsewhere

If you have never worked in someone else's restaurant, you are not ready to start one of your own. A special personality is needed to run a restaurant. Previous work in someone else's restaurant is an excellent—and a very inexpensive—way to gain restaurant expertise, learn from others' mistakes, and find out if you possess the basic ingredient for successful ownership: the right kind of personality.

## Choose a Good Location

A restaurant owner must find property that complements the restaurant's layout and operation. Therefore, it is necessary to consider the following basic questions before choosing a specific site:

What kind of food will be served?
What is the general price range of food items?
What type of service (fast-food, self-service, cafeteria, counter, table service) will be offered?
What specific menu items will be served?
What kind of atmosphere is desired?
Who is the anticipated clientele?
What cooking methods will be used?
What size staff is necessary?
What kind of inventory is required?
What hours will the restaurant operate?
What are the projected sales?
What amount of food should be prepared on-site?

## *Market Study*

Adequate market research can help the prospective owner determine whether his or her ideas match the needs of the locale. A good market study will reveal who the potential customers are, what percentage of the population they represent, and the competition that exists. It also will help determine the business traffic patterns by hours of the day, days of the week, and weekday versus weekend. This knowledge will help the prospective owner supply the needs of customers and compete with existing restaurants. It will also be a big help when seeking funding from a financial institution.

The U.S. Census of Population provides demographic profiles, income levels, and housing patterns by geographic segments, right down to city blocks. The local chamber of commerce and the National Restaurant Association information service and library in Washington, D.C., have additional market research data.

## *Selecting a Specific Site*

Location is perhaps the most deciding factor for a restaurant's success. Leave no stone unturned in scrutinizing the proper site. Ask yourself the following questions:

Can the site be seen from the street?
Are parking arrangements available?
What types of businesses are nearby?
Do taxicabs and/or buses come by the area?
What are the peak hours of traffic?
Are there plans for growth in the area?
How many households are in the area?

Sources of helpful information include the Department of Commerce, the Small Business Association, real estate agencies, restaurant consultants, accountants, bankers, and insurance agents.

### Researching Codes, Ordinances, and Permits

Learn everything possible about the laws covering restaurant businesses in the area. This will reduce the possibility of being shut down or slapped with heavy fines after the restaurant opens. Some common codes include fire, health, parking, occupancy, garbage, sewage, and loading zone.

In addition, a number of licenses are necessary before opening a restaurant. Some states require a business license or a sales tax license. A fictitious name license or DBAS (doing business as . . .) may be needed if the restaurant is operated under a name different from the owner's. If alcoholic beverages are on the menu, a liquor and beer and wine license is needed.

## Organize Your Restaurant

A well-organized restaurant will help ensure success because it will be well run and equipped to handle any unforeseen circumstances. From the appearance of the space, both indoors and out, to the items on the menu, there are a variety of important factors to consider when you set up your restaurant. However, perhaps the two most important are the items you offer your patrons to eat and how your kitchen is equipped to handle the preparation of them.

### Planning the Menu

Planning the menu means deciding what items to offer and what price to ask. Restaurants that offer a limited menu and still do a high volume of business will be the most profitable. However, a limited menu sometimes restricts the restaurant's appeal and image.

Many new operations have failed because of overpricing. A general rule often used in the restaurant industry is that a menu price should not be more than double or triple the wholesale food cost.

A well-thought-out menu can serve as a guide for ordering, purchasing, and estimating income. A menu also will help determine the layout of the kitchen, the level of skill the staff needs, the level of service necessary, the amount of storage space needed, and what special equipment must be purchased.

### *Planning the Kitchen*

The kitchen is a very important part of any restaurant, and careful planning of the kitchen can help ensure smooth operation. A good kitchen plan includes the following:

- Ample workspace for food preparation
- Adequate space to pass food from the cooks to the food servers
- Sufficient aisle space for food servers to deliver the food to the patrons
- A cleanup center for washing dishes and disposing of garbage
- A separate area for inventory delivery
- An area for storage of foodstuffs and linens
- Proper ventilation and lighting
- Reliable equipment that is easy to maintain, clean, and repair

## Establish a Solid Business

Many people find the business side of owning their own restaurant, including the legal and financial aspects, among the most daunting of the many things one must consider before starting a business. However, with the proper research and education you should be able to establish a solid business. Securing adequate financing, banking on the reliability of an established franchise, and using the expertise of lawyers are just a few ways to ensure success.

### Secure Adequate Financing

One of the major causes of restaurant failure is insufficient financing. Don't underestimate common start-up costs. These costs can include wiring, plumbing, painting, labor, materials, kitchen fixtures and equipment, furniture, an initial lease deposit or down payment on property, remodeling or improvements, license payments, utility and insurance deposits, initial food inventory, initial advertising, and consultant fees for experts such as lawyers, accountants, publicists, kitchen designers, and menu designers.

### Consider Franchise Opportunities

A restaurant franchised by reputable chains has an 80 percent survival rate, compared to the 20 percent survival rate of other restaurants. Therefore, many first-time restaurateurs prefer to go this route. In recent years, it has become increasingly difficult to break into the franchise business, but it can be done.

Franchising is a form of licensing by which the owner or the franchiser obtains distribution through affiliated dealers called the franchisees. Franchise agreements call for the parent company to give an independent businessperson rights to a successful restaurant concept and trademark as well as assistance in organizing, training, merchandising, and management. The franchisee pays the company a franchise fee and monthly royalties for these rights and assistance.

Franchisers look for people who are eager to become independent operators but who will conform to guidelines from company headquarters. Before becoming a franchisee, one should carefully investigate the backgrounds and current business practices of the franchiser. A reputable franchise company should provide the following:

- A site—usually a freestanding building that is leased to the franchisee
- Exclusive territorial rights
- Any exclusively developed equipment
- Licensed use of trademark, inventory system, exclusive recipes, and techniques
- Training courses and operations manuals
- Continuing operations assistance for a specified percentage of gross sales
- Inspections by company supervisors who will evaluate the operation
- Equipment, suppliers, and advertising

## *Hire a Lawyer*

A lawyer is a safeguard to ensure that the franchisee's interests are protected. Remember, the cost of legal advice at the outset will always be less than the cost of later representation to solve problems that could have been avoided in the beginning.

Part of the lawyer's job includes ascertaining the length of contract, royalty charges, fixed charges, purchasing requirements, quotas, arbitration privileges, contract termination, and how the company can terminate the franchisee.

## Build a Good Staff

No company or business succeeds with the merits of just one person alone, and nowhere is this more evident than in the restaurant industry. Operating a restaurant is not a one-person show. A good staff is critical to success.

Recruiting, interviewing, hiring, and training the proper people can be a time-consuming and nerve-racking process, but time well invested in the beginning will pay off substantially in the end.

## Paying Employees

According to the National Restaurant Association, restaurants covered by the federal minimum wage law, which is also known as the Fair Labor Standards Act (FLSA), must pay hourly employees at least $5.15 an hour and tipped employees a cash wage or at least $2.13 an hour. However, you may be required to pay a rate higher than that. States may set their own wage rates, and when they do, employers who are covered by the FLSA must pay whichever rate, state or federal, that is most favorable to the employee. Before you establish your wage rates, you should seek the counsel of an attorney.

## A General Business Education Is Useful

It is not necessary to have an advanced degree or even a high school diploma to work in the restaurant industry, but a college education makes it easier to move up the career ladder quickly and achieve your professional and financial goals. A general business degree will help greatly in running your own restaurant.

# 9

## EDUCATIONAL REQUIREMENTS
## AND RESOURCES

THE MORE TRAINING and education an individual has, the better the opportunity to begin employment at a higher level of income and responsibility. This well-known fact applies to every industry, including the restaurant business. However, the restaurant industry subscribes to the adage that experience is a great teacher. Therefore, no one has to drop out of the running because of lack of education or specific training.

More than in many other industries, restaurants offer entry-level career opportunities in great variety. The ambitious, hardworking, and career-minded individual is sure to find a route to the top in this growing industry. Thus, for the recent high school graduate who plans an immediate career start, a restaurant career is well worth considering. It is also ideal for individuals who wish to begin or change careers later in life.

Most restaurant operations are willing to invest time and money in training newcomers to the field. Once an individual has gained a sound base of knowledge, it is possible for him or her to move upward into jobs with more responsibility and better pay.

## Opportunities in High School

Students who are still in high school can accelerate their restaurant career development by taking food-service courses offered in high schools or vocational schools. These courses, depending on the type and number taken, can give the graduate an advantage when seeking employment. Also, part-time work in a restaurant while still in high school can be a valuable aid.

The National Restaurant Association and the American Hotel and Lodging Association formed an educational partnership called the Hospitality Business Alliance (HBA) to create a nationwide system of high school hospitality courses linked with mentored worksite experiences.

Under the HBA/ProStart School-to-Career Initiative, more than twenty-four thousand high school juniors and seniors are now studying restaurant and food-service management at more than six hundred schools in thirty-six states, according to a report by the National Restaurant Association Educational Foundation (NRAEF).

The ProStart curriculum is a two-year curriculum designed to teach students the management skills needed for a career in the restaurant and food-service industry. The students participate in paid internships where industry managers mentor them. When students meet academic standards and complete a checklist of competencies, they are awarded the ProStart National Certificate of Achievement, which signifies they are well qualified to enter the industry workforce.

The NRAEF offers $2,000 scholarships to certificate holders to help further their education.

# Junior and Community Colleges

One of the richest sources of new management talent in the restaurant industry is found in junior and community colleges that offer associate degrees in various aspects of food service. Hundreds of jobs are open to graduates with this training.

Two-year college programs in food service pave the way for graduates to undertake beginning administrative and supervisory jobs in nearly any type of restaurant operation. There are a wide variety of courses available at junior and community colleges. They include:

- Food purchasing and storage
- Food preparation
- Menu planning
- Equipment purchasing and layout
- Personnel management and job analysis
- Food standards and sanitation
- Diet therapy
- Catering
- Beverage control
- Food cost accounting
- Record keeping

In addition to these courses, a number of general courses, designed to broaden the student's knowledge and outlook on the restaurant industry, may include the following:

- Communication skills
- Psychology
- Sociology
- Economics
- Chemistry

- Nutrition
- Physical education

The advantage of many community and junior college programs is that they are less expensive than other college programs and they combine classroom work with practical job experience in part-time restaurant jobs. Many restaurant owners support local college programs by providing part-time employment for students and also career opportunities for graduates.

## Four-Year Universities or Colleges

The restaurant industry's need for graduates of four-year college programs in management has never been filled. A large number of management and management-training positions are open in all segments of the industry, including the following:

- Assistant manager
- Food production supervisor
- Purchasing agent
- Food cost accountant
- Food-service director
- Director of recipe development
- Sales manager
- Banquet manager
- Catering manager

Undergraduate programs include:

- Basic and advanced courses in food preparation
- Specialized courses in restaurant accounting, catering, management, and sanitation

- General courses in economics, law, marketing, cost control, and finance

Many four-year colleges require summer work in restaurants as well. Graduates of four-year programs can receive a bachelor's degree in restaurant management.

## Training in the Restaurant Industry

The restaurant industry is a very competitive business. Therefore, restaurant employers offer extensive training to their workers to ensure high levels of customer satisfaction. These training programs improve restaurant business and at the same time help unskilled workers develop career potential.

Workers are trained not only for the jobs they are hired for but also for the positions to which they would like to advance. Through such programs as apprenticeships, internships, mentoring, and management development initiatives, employees have the opportunity to explore their interest in and suitability for careers in the restaurant industry. Programs of this nature offer workers with great potential but limited skills a supportive environment where they can develop the expertise needed to enhance their career options.

### *McDonald's Hamburger University*

McDonald's Corporation, the largest restaurant organization in the world with more than thirty thousand restaurants doing business in 119 countries around the globe, has a worldwide management-training center in Oak Brook, Illinois. It is called Hamburger University, and its main purpose is to instruct McDonald's personnel in the various aspects of its business.

Hamburger University offers a crew development program, where employees learn the basic operations of restaurant performance while always focusing on the customer; a restaurant management course, where students develop key skills to successfully develop a restaurant business plan; a mid-management program where McDonald's consultants, department heads, and franchisees are skilled in the competencies needed to effectively lead and consult with restaurant staff around the world; and an executive development program, where McDonald's officers enhance their leadership skills needed to support employee, owner/operator, and customer growth worldwide.

Nearly six thousand students each year attend Hamburger University, each with the goal of advancing his or her career. By 2003, Hamburger University had graduated more than seventy thousand people who now manage McDonald's restaurants.

The McDonald's Corporation sums up its management training philosophy in this way:

> From our employees, we demand enthusiasm, hard work, stick-to-the-basics, and complete dedication to the objectives of the organization. Our company provides training opportunities at all levels from trainee to executive. All of it begins with the knowledge and skills from the operating restaurant level. There is no progress for those who fail to measure up, and there is no ceiling for those who master the successive tasks.

### And Burger King, Too

Burger King Corporation also has a training school to help managers advance their careers. Formerly known as Whopper College, it is now called Burger King University (BKU) and is located in Miami, Florida, at the corporation's headquarters.

Assistant managers receive training in restaurants and regional training centers throughout the country. As part of final training, before becoming a functional regional manager, employees attend BKU in Miami for one or two weeks to gain administrative and financial training. Total training lasts ten to twelve weeks.

Training covers the operational, technical, marketing, financial, and administrative aspects of the industry. Some of the subjects students are taught include:

- Basic bookkeeping and accounting procedures
- Sanitation standards
- How to properly maintain grounds
- How to promote programs
- How to identify problems with machinery
- How to identify viable work applicants
- How to schedule personnel
- How to order inventory
- How many cash registers to have open
- How to delegate responsibility
- How to anticipate patronage
- How to prepare food products to ensure consistency from location to location

Founded with one restaurant in Miami, Florida, in 1954, Burger King and its franchises in 2003 were operating 11,350 restaurants in all fifty states and fifty-seven countries and territories worldwide. Ninety-one percent of Burger King restaurants are owned and operated by independent franchisees.

## Pizza Hut's Minority Mentor Program

Pizza Hut, Inc., headquartered in Wichita, Kansas, conducts a year-long program for newly hired minority and women managers. In this program, new managers are placed with personnel two levels above their rank who serve as role models. Informal contact is made every two weeks during the year to provide indoctrination into the corporate environment and to discuss problems. The mentors guide, counsel, protect, and sometimes promote the development of the junior members. Role models may be in a different department from the new manager in order to provide broader exposure to the corporation.

Pizza Hut was established in 1958. There are a total of 5,901 franchises in the United States and 3,571 in foreign countries. Nearly 25 percent are corporate-owned outlets.

# U.S. Schools Offering Hospitality Programs

IN THE PAST, many restaurant employees learned their occupation by starting at the most entry-level position at the establishment and working their way up to a more responsible and higher-paying job. For many, this process took a long time. Now there are numerous academic programs designed to provide the training essential for nearly any job an aspiring worker seeks.

Even for the worker who fills entry-level jobs that require no prior experience, promotion to higher-level jobs is gained faster when education is added to experience. Individuals trying to advance into top and middle management positions can enhance their prospects by preparing themselves educationally. In many instances, education may be substituted for experience on a year-for-year basis.

Large restaurants and restaurant chains are currently placing more emphasis on education and formal training as the fast pace and competition in the business community continue. Recruiters from these restaurants go to colleges to interview students graduating with degrees in the field.

The information in this appendix is taken from an extensive survey conducted by the National Restaurant Association and the National Institute for the Food Service Industry. The list included here contains only a sample of schools in each state that offer hospitality education programs.

Visit the website provided for additional information on the school of your choice.

In most cases, the title of the program or department is included with each school's listing. Although programs vary greatly, there appear to be two general categories of programs: one in the area of hospitality (hotel and restaurant management) and the other in the area of culinary arts and commercial cooking. Many schools offer both.

Contact a school directly for more details and for the most current information on its program.

### *Alabama*

Auburn University
Hotel and Restaurant Management
School of Human Sciences
Department of Nutrition and Food Science
humsci.auburn.edu

Bishop State Technical College, Carver Campus
Commercial Foodservice
bscc.cc.al.us

Faulkner State Community College
faulkner.cc.al.us

Jefferson State Community College
Hospitality Management
jscc.cc.al.us

Lawson State Community College
Commercial Food Services/Culinary Arts
ls.cc.al.us

Tuskegee University
Department of Home Economics
Hospitality Management Program
http://agriculture.tusk.edu

The University of Alabama
Restaurant and Hospitality Management
College of Human Environmental Sciences
ches.ua.edu

Wallace State Community College
Commercial Foods
wallacestate.edu

## *Alaska*

Alaska Pacific University
Travel and Hospitality Management
alaskapacific.edu

Alaska Vocational Technical Center
Culinary Arts and Sciences Department
http://avtec.labor.state.ak.us

University of Alaska, Anchorage
Culinary Arts
http://hosting.uaa.alaska.edu

University of Alaska, Fairbanks
Travel Industry Management Program
School of Management
uaf.edu

## *Arizona*

The Art Institute of Phoenix
Culinary Arts
aipx.aii.edu

Northern Arizona University
School of Hotel and Restaurant Management
nau.edu

Phoenix College
Culinary Studies and Foodservice Administration
pc.maricopa.edu

Scottsdale Community College
Hospitality Management/Culinary Arts
sc.maricopa.edu

Scottsdale Culinary Institute
scichefs.com

University of Arizona
Department of Nutritional Service
http://ag.arizona.edu

## *Arkansas*

Arkansas Tech University
Hotel and Restaurant Management
School of Business
http://syssci.atu.edu

University of Arkansas at Pine Bluff
Restaurant Foodservice Management
uapb.edu

## *California*

Alliant International University
Hotel and Restaurant Management Program
Tourism Management Program
alliant.edu

American River College
Culinary Arts and Hospitality Management
arc.losrios.edu

Cabrillo College
Culinary Arts
cabrillo.edu

California Culinary Academy
Professional Chef Program
baychef.com

California School of Culinary Arts
calchef.com

California State Polytechnic University, Pomona
The Collins School of Hospitality Management
csupomona.edu

California State University, Chico
Foodservice Administration
Nutrition and Food Services
csuchico.edu

California State University, Long Beach
Hospitality Foodservice and Hotel Management Program
csulb.edu

Chaffey College
Hotel and Foodservice Management
chaffey.edu

Chapman University
Department of Food Science and Nutrition
chapman.edu

City College of San Francisco
Hotel and Restaurant Department
ccsf.edu

College of the Canyons
Hotel and Restaurant Management
coc.cc.ca.us

College of the Desert
desert.cc.ca.us

College of the Sequoias
Nutrition and Foods
http://zeus.sequoias.cc.ca.us

Columbia College
Hospitality Management
http://columbia.yosemite.cc.ca.us

Cypress College
Hospitality Management
cypresscollege.edu

Diablo Valley College
Hotel and Restaurant Management
dvc.edu

Glendale Community College
Foodservice Management
glendale.cc.ca.us

Los Angeles Trade-Technical College
Chef Training/Restaurant Management
lattc.cc.ca.us

Mission College
Nutrition and Dietary Services
missioncollege.org

Orange Coast College
Culinary Arts
occ.cccd.edu

San Francisco State University
Hospitality Management
sfsu.edu

San Joaquin Delta College
Culinary Arts Department
deltacollege.org

San Jose State University
Hospitality Management
hospitality.sjsu.edu

Santa Barbara City College
Hotel, Restaurant, and Culinary
sbcc.edu

Skyline College
Hospitality Program
skylinecollege.net

University of San Francisco
Hospitality Management Program
csulb.edu

## *Colorado*

Colorado Mountain College
Culinary Arts
coloradomtn.edu

Colorado State University
Restaurant and Resort Management
http://leeds.colorado.edu

Cook Street School of Fine Cooking
https://clients.caseshare.com/cookstreet

Cooking School of the Rockies
Culinary Arts
cookingschoolrockies.com/home.html

Fort Lewis College
Tourism and Resort Management
dcb.du.edu

Johnson and Wales University
Culinary Facilities
jwu.edu/denver/index.htm

Metropolitan State College of Denver
Hospitality, Meeting, and Travel
mscd.edu

Pikes Peak Community College
Culinary Arts/Food Management
ppcc.cccoes.edu

Pueblo Community College
Culinary Arts
pueblocc.edu

University of Colorado at Boulder
Tourism Management Program
http://leeds.colorado.edu

University of Denver
School of Hotel/Motel, Hospitality Management, and Tourism
dcb.du.edu

## *Connecticut*

Connecticut Culinary Institute
ctculinary.com

Manchester Community Technical College
Hospitality Management
mctc.commnet.edu

Naugatuck Valley Community Technical College
Hospitality Management
http://155.43.16.5/hospman

University of Connecticut
Department of Nutritional Sciences
canr.uconn.edu

University of New Haven
Hotel, Restaurant, Tourism Administration
newhaven.edu

## *Delaware*

Delaware State University
Hotel and Restaurant Management
dsc.edu

Delaware Technical and Community College
School of Hotel, Restaurant, and Hospitality Management
dtcc.edu

The University of Delaware
Hotel, Restaurant, and Institutional Management
Culinary Arts, Foodservice Management
udel.edu

## *District of Columbia*

The George Washington University
International Institute of Tourism Studies
gwutourism.org

Howard University
Hospitality Management
howard.edu

## *Florida*

Art Institute of Fort Lauderdale
Culinary Arts
aifl.artinstitutes.edu

Atlantic Vocational Technical Center
Culinary Arts
atlantictechcenter.com

Bethune Cookman College
Hospitality Management
cookman.edu

Daytona Beach Community College
Hospitality Management
http://faculty.dbcc.cc.fl.us

Florida A & M University
Hospitality Management Program
famu.edu

Florida Community College
Restaurant Management
fccj.org

Florida Culinary Institute
floridaculinary.com

Florida International University
Hospitality Management, Hotel, and Food Service Management
http://hospitality.fiu.edu

Florida State University
The Dedman School of Hospitality
cob.fsu.edu

Gulf Coast Community College
Culinary and Hospitality Management
http://culinary.gc.cc.fl.us

Hillsborough Community College
Hotel and Resort Management/Chef Apprentice Training
hccfl.edu

Johnson and Wales University
Culinary Arts
jwu.edu

Lynn University
Hospitality and Tourism
lynn.edu

Pensacola Junior College
Hospitality/Culinary Management
pjc.cc.fl.us

Pinellas Technical Education Center, Clearwater
Commercial Foods/Culinary Arts
ptecclw.pinellas.k12.fl.us/programs.htm

Saint Leo College
Division of Professional Studies
Hospitality and Tourism Management
saintleo.edu

Saint Thomas University
Tourism and Hospitality Management
stu.edu

Schiller International University, Florida
Hotel Management
schiller.edu

University of Central Florida
Hospitality Management
dce.ucf.edu

University of Florida
Food Science and Human Nutrition Department
http://fshn.ifas.ufl.edu

## Georgia

The Art Institute of Atlanta
Culinary Arts
aia.artinstitutes.edu/programs

East Central Technical College
eastcentral.tec.ga.us

Georgia Southern University
Restaurant, Hotel, and Institutional Administration
http://www2.gasou.edu

Georgia State University
Cecil B. Day School of Hospitality Administration
http://robinson.gsu.edu

Morris Brown College
Hospitality Administration
morrisbrown.edu

Savannah Technical College
Culinary Arts
http://web.savannah.tec.ga.us

University of Georgia
Foods and Nutrition
fcs.uga.edu

## *Hawaii*

Brigham Young University, Hawaii
Hospitality and Tourism Management
http://bus.byuh.edu

Hawaii Community College
Foodservice Program
http://web.hawcc.hawaii.edu

Hawaii Pacific University
Foodservice, Hospitality
College of Business Administration
http://programs.kcc.hawaii.edu/fshe/foodserv.htm

Kapiolani Community College
Foodservice and Hospitality Education
http://programs.kcc.hawaii.edu/fshe

Kauai Community College
Culinary Arts
kauaicc.hawaii.edu

Leeward Community College
Culinary Institute of the Pacific
Foodservice Program
http://emedia.leeward.hawaii.edu/foodservice/default.htm

Maui Community College
Food Service Program
http://mauicc.hawaii.edu

University of Hawaii at Manoa
Hospitality, Tourism Management
School of Travel Industry Management
tim.hawaii.edu

## *Idaho*

Boise State University
Culinary Arts
http://selland.boisestate.edu

College of Southern Idaho
Hotel-Restaurant Management
csi.edu

Idaho State University
Culinary Arts
School of Applied Technology
isu.edu

North Idaho College
Culinary Arts
nic.edu

University of Idaho
Food Science and Toxicology
Holm Research Center
ag.uidaho.edu

## *Illinois*

Chicago State University
Hospitality Management
College of Business
csu.edu

Chopping Block Cooking School
thechoppingblock.net

College of DuPage
Hospitality Management
cod.edu

The Cooking and Hospitality Institute of Chicago
Culinary Arts
chicnet.org

Eastern Illinois University
Hospitality Services
College of Applied Sciences
eiu.edu

Elgin Community College
Hospitality Management
elgin.cc.il.us

Harper College
Hospitality Industry
harpercollege.edu

Illinois Institute of Art, Chicago
Culinary Arts
ilic.artinstitutes.edu

John Wood Community College
Food Service Programs
jwcc.edu

Joliet Junior College
Hotel, Restaurant, and Food Service Management, Culinary Arts
jjc.cc.il.us

Kendall College
Hospitality Management, Culinary Arts
kendall.edu

Kennedy-King College
Food Management
ccc.edu

Lincoln Land Community College
Applied Sciences Department
llcc.cc.il.us

Moraine Valley Community College
Hotel/Restaurant Management
morainevalley.edu

Northern Illinois University
Food Systems Administration: Dietetics, Nutrition,
    and Food Systems
College of Professional Studies
Department of Human and Family Resources
fcns.niu.edu

Rend Lake College
Culinary Arts Management
rlc.cc.il.us

Robert Morris College
Institute of Culinary Arts
robertmorris.edu

Roosevelt University
Hospitality Management
roosevelt.edu

South Western Illinois College
Hospitality/Foodservice Management
southwestern.cc.il.us

Southern Illinois University, Carbondale
Hotel, Restaurant, and Travel Administration
College of Agriculture
c/o Food and Nutrition
Department of Animal Science, Food, and Nutrition
siu.edu

Triton College
Hospitality Institute
triton.cc.il.us

University of Illinois at Urbana, Champaign
Restaurant/Hospitality Management
fshn.uiuc.edu

Western Illinois University
Food Service and Lodging Management Program
College of Applied Sciences
Department of Home Economics
wiu.edu

## *Indiana*

Atterbury Job Corps Center
Food Services
ajcc.org

Ball State University
Food Management
Department of Home Economics
bsu.edu

Indiana Career and Postsecondary Advancement Center
Hospitality Management
icpac.indiana.edu

Purdue University
Restaurant, Hotel, Institutional, and Tourism Management (RHIT)
cfs.purdue.edu

Purdue University, Calumet
Restaurant, Hotel, Institutional, and Tourism Management
calumet.purdue.edu

Vincennes University
Hotel and Restaurant Management
vinu.edu

## *Iowa*

Des Moines Area Community College
Hospitality Management
dmacc.cc.ia.us

Indian Hills Community College
Culinary Arts
ihcc.cc.ia.us

Iowa State University
Hotel, Restaurant, and Institution Management
fcs.iastate.edu

Iowa Western Community College
Culinary Arts
iwcc.cc.ia.us

Kirkwood Community College
Culinary Arts
kirkwood.cc.ia.us

## Kansas

Johnson County Community College
Hospitality Management
jccc.net

Kansas State University
Hotel and Restaurant Management and Dietetics
humec.ksu.edu

Wichita Area Vocational Technical College
Foodservice Education
wichitatech.com

## Kentucky

Bowling Green Technical College
Culinary Arts
bgtc.net

Morehead State University
Hotel, Restaurant, and Institutional Management
College of Applied Sciences and Technology
Department of Human Sciences
morehead-st.edu

Sullivan College
National Center for Hospitality Studies
sullivan.edu

Transylvania University
Hotel, Restaurant, and Tourism Administration
transy.edu

University of Kentucky
Hospitality Management
Human Environmental Sciences
uky.edu

West Kentucky State Vocational Technical School
Culinary Arts
wkytech.com/food.html

Western Kentucky University
Hotel, Restaurant, and Tourism Management
College of Education and Behavioral Sciences
Home Economics and Consumer Sciences
wku.edu

## *Louisiana*

Bossier Parish Community College
Culinary Arts
bpcc.cc.la.us

Delgado Community College
Culinary Arts Department
dcc.edu

Grambling State University
Hotel and Restaurant Management
College of Science and Technology
gram.edu

Louisiana Technical College
Culinary Arts and Occupations
theltc.net

Nicholls State University
Chef John Folse Culinary Institute
nich.edu

Sclafani Cooking School
sclafanicookingschool.com

Southern University and A & M College
subr.edu

University of New Orleans
School of Hotel, Restaurant, and Tourism Administration
College of Business Administration
uno.edu

## *Maine*

Central Maine Technical College
Culinary Arts
cmtc.net

Eastern Maine Technical College
Business and Industry
emcc.edu

Husson College
Hospitality Management Program
husson.edu

Southern Maine Technical College
Culinary Arts and Hotel, Motel, Restaurant Management
smtc.net

Thomas College
Hotel and Restaurant Management
thomas.edu

University of Maine, Bangor
Hotel/Restaurant/Tourism Management
School of Business
fsn.umaine.edu

University of Maine, Orona
Department of Food Science and Human Nutrition
fsn.umaine.edu

Washington County Technical College
Food and Hospitality Department
wctc.org

York County Community College
Culinary Arts
yctc.net

## Maryland

Allegany College of Maryland
Hospitality/Foodservice Management
ac.cc.md.us

Anne Arundel Community College
Hotel/Restaurant Management
aacc.cc.md.us

Baltimore International Culinary College
Professional Cooking, Professional Baking and Pastry, Innkeeping,
Restaurant Management
bic.edu

Morgan State University
Hospitality Management
morgan.edu

University of Maryland, College Park
Nutrition and Food Science
agnr.umd.edu

University of Maryland, Eastern Shore
Hotel and Restaurant Management
School of Professional Studies
umes.edu

## *Massachusetts*

Berkshire Community College
Culinary Arts
http://cc.berkshire.org

Boston University
School of Hospitality Administration
bu.edu

Bunker Hill Community College
Hospitality Management
bhcc.mass.edu

The Cambridge School of Culinary Arts
cambridgeculinary.com

Endicott College
Hospitality Division
Liberal and Professional Arts College
endicott.edu

Framingham State College
Food Science and Nutrition
Department of Home Economics
framingham.edu

Holyoke Community College
Nutrition and Food
hcc.mass.edu

International School of Culinary Arts
culinaryschool.com

Lasell College
Hotel and Travel/Tourism Administration
lasell.edu

Massachusetts Bay Community College
Hospitality Management
mbcc.mass.edu

Massasoit Community College
Culinary Arts
massasoit.mass.edu

Newbury College
Hospitality Management, Culinary Arts
newbury.edu

Simmons College
Nutrition
simmons.edu

University of Massachusetts, Amherst
Department of Hotel, Restaurant, and Travel Administration
College of Food and Natural Resources
umass.edu

## *Michigan*

Central Michigan University
Hospitality Services
Marketing and Hospitality Services Administration
http://mkt.cba.cmich.edu

Ferris State University
Foodservice/Hospitality Management
ferris.edu

Grand Rapids Community College
Hospitality Management
grcc.cc.mi.us

Henry Ford Community College
Hospitality Management
henryford.cc.mi.us

Kirtland Community College
Hospitality Program
kirtland.cc.mi.us

Lansing Community College
Hospitality Program
lansing.cc.mi.us

Macomb Community College
Culinary Arts
macomb.cc.mi.us

Michigan State University
School of Hospitality Business
The Eli Broad College of Business
bus.msu.edu

Monroe County Community College
Culinary Skills and Management
monroeccc.edu

Mott Community College
Food Service Management
mcc.edu

North Central Michigan College
Dietetics and Nutrition
wccnet.org

Northern Michigan University
College of Technology and Applied Sciences
Foodservice Department
nmu.edu

Northwestern Michigan College
Hospitality Management
nmc.edu/business

Northwood University
Hotel/Restaurant Management
northwood.edu

Oakland Community College
Hospitality/Culinary Arts
occ.cc.mi.us

Siena Heights College
Hotel, Restaurant, and Institutional Management
sienahts.edu

Washtenaw Community College
Culinary and Hospitality Management
wccnet.org

## *Minnesota*

Alexandria Technical College
Hospitality Management
alextech.org

The Arts Institute International, Minnesota
Culinary Arts
aim.artinstitutes.edu

Byerly's School of Culinary Arts
byerlys.com

Hennepin Technical Center
Restaurant Management
hennepintech.edu

Hibbing Community College
Culinary Arts
hcc.mnscu.edu/programs

Le Cordon Bleu Culinary Program at Brown Institute
culinary-bi.com

Minnesota State University
Foods and Nutrition
mankato.msus.edu

Normandale Community College
Hospitality Management
normandale.mnscu.edu

Northwest Technical College, Moorhead
Hospitality Management
ntcmn.edu

St. Paul Technical College
Restaurant and Hotel Cookery
saintpaul.edu

South Central Technical College
Culinary Arts
sctc.mnscu.edu

University of Minnesota, Crookston
Hotel, Restaurant, and Institutional Management
crk.umn.edu

## *Mississippi*

Alcorn State University
Nutrition and Dietetics
alcorn.edu

East Mississippi Community College
Hotel and Restaurant Management
emcc.cc.ms.us

Hinds Community College
Restaurant Management
hindscc.edu

Meridian Community College
Restaurant and Hotel Management
mcc.cc.ms.us

Mississippi Gulf Coast Community College
Foodservice Department
http://www2.mgccc.cc.ms.us

Mississippi State University
Food, Nutrition, and Dietetics
msstate.edu

Mississippi University for Women
Culinary Arts
muw.edu

## *Missouri*

Central Missouri State University
Hotel and Restaurant Administration
Department of Human Environmental Sciences
cmsu.edu

College of the Ozarks
Hotel and Restaurant Management
cofo.edu/ozarks.htm

East Central College
Hospitality Management
ecc.cc.mo.us

Mineral Area College
Hospitality
mac.cc.mo.us

St. Louis Community College at Forest Park
Hospitality Management
stlcc.cc.mo.us

Southeast Missouri State University
Human Environmental Studies
http://www5.semo.edu/hes

Southwest Missouri State University
Hospitality and Restaurant Administration
Health and Applied Sciences
smsu.edu

University of Missouri, Columbia
Hotel and Restaurant Management
College of Agriculture, Food, and Natural Resources
fse.missouri.edu

## *Montana*

Blackfeet Community College
Hospitality Department
bfcc.org

University of Montana College of Technology
Foodservice Management, Culinary Arts
cte.umt.edu

## *Nebraska*

Central Community College
Hotel, Motel, Restaurant Management
cccneb.edu

Chadron State College
Food Management
csc.edu

Metropolitan Community College
Foodservice Management
http://business.mccneb.edu

Southeast Community College
Foodservice Management
college.sccm.cc.ne.us

University of Nebraska, Lincoln
Restaurant Management
Home Economics
Nutritional Science and Dietetics
unl.edu

Western Nebraska Community College
Dietetics
wncc.net

## *Nevada*

Community College of Southern Nevada
Culinary Arts
ccsn.nevada.edu

Nothing to It Culinary Center
nothingtoit.com

Sierra Nevada College, Lake Tahoe
Hotel and Restaurant Management
sierranevada.edu

Truckee Meadows Community College
Foodservice Technology
tmcc.edu

University of Nevada, Las Vegas
William F. Harrah College of Hotel Administration
unlv.edu

University of Nevada, Reno
Department of Nutrition
unr.edu

## *New Hampshire*

McIntosh College
Atlantic Culinary Academy
http://atlanticculinary.com

New Hampshire College
Hospitality, Tourism, and Culinary Management
nhc.edu

New Hampshire Community Technical College, Berlin
Culinary Arts
berlin.tec.nh.us

New Hampshire Community Technical College, Laconia
Restaurant, Lodging, and Conference Management
laconia.tec.nh.us

Southern New Hampshire University
School of Hospitality
snhu.edu

A Taste of the Mountains Cooking School
Culinary Arts
virtualcities.com

University of New Hampshire
Hospitality Management, Dietetics
http://orbit.unh.edu

## *New Jersey*

Atlantic Community College
Academy of Culinary Arts
atlantic.edu

Bergen Community College
Hotel-Restaurant Management
atlantic.edu

Burlington County College
Hospitality Management
http://staff.bcc.edu

Camden County College
Dietetics Technology
camdencc.edu

College of St. Elizabeth
Foods and Nutrition
cse.edu

Cumberland County College
Hospitality and Tourism Management
cccnj.net

Essex County College
Hospitality Management
essex.edu

Fairleigh Dickinson University
School of Hotel, Restaurant, and Tourism Management
fdu.edu

Gloucester County College
Hospitality Management
gccnj.edu

Hudson County Community College
Culinary Arts
hudson.cc.nj.us

Mercer County Community College
Hotel, Restaurant, and Institution Management
hudson.cc.nj.us

Middlesex County College
Hotel, Restaurant, and Institution Management
HRI Department
middlesex.cc.nj.us

Raritan Valley Community College
Hospitality Management
raritanval.edu

Rutgers University
Food Science Department
http://nutrition.rutgers.edu

Thomas Edison State College
Dietetic Sciences
tesc.edu

Union County Vocational Technical School
Culinary Arts, Baking Program
ucc.edu

## *New Mexico*

Albuquerque Vocational Technical Institute
Hospitality and Tourism
tvi.cc.nm.us

Dona Ana Branch Community College
Hospitality Services
http://dabcc-www.nmsu.edu

New Mexico State University
Hospitality and Tourism Services
Agriculture and Home Economics
nmsu.edu

Santa Fe School of Cooking
santafeschoolofcooking.com

## *New York*

Adirondack Community College
Foodservice Program
sunyacc.edu

Alfred State College
Culinary Arts
alfredtech.edu

The Art Institute of New York City
Culinary Arts
http://iris.nyit.edu/culinary

Broome Community College
Hospitality Management
sunybroome.edu

Cornell University
Hotel Administration
cornell.edu

The Culinary Institute of America
Culinary Arts, Baking, and Pastry Arts
ciachef.edu

Daemen College
Division of Business and Commerce
Transportation and Travel Management
nysaes.cornell.edu

Delhi College of Technology
Hospitality Management
delhi.edu

Dutchess Community College
Hospitality and Tourism
sunydutchess.edu

Erie Community College, North Campus
Foodservice Administration/Restaurant Management
sunyerie.edu

French Culinary Institute
frenchculinary.com

Fulton Montgomery Community College
Foodservice Management
http://fmcc.suny.edu

Jefferson Community College
Hospitality Management
sunyjefferson.edu

Keuka College
Food, Hotel, and Resort Management
keuka.edu

Mohawk Valley Community College, Rome Campus
Foodservice/Hospitality Management
mvcc.edu

Monroe Community College
Food, Hotel, and Tourism Management
monroecc.edu

Nassau Community College
Hotel Technology Administration
sunynassau.edu

New York City Technical College
Hotel and Restaurant Management
nyctc.cuny.edu

New York Institute of Technology, Central Islip Campus
Hotel/Restaurant Administration and Culinary Arts
http://iris.nyit.edu

New York University
Hotel, Restaurant, and Food Management
scps.nyu.edu/departments/index.jsp

Niagara County Community College
Professional Chef
sunyniagara.cc.ny.us

Niagara University
Institute of Travel, Hotel, and Restaurant Administration
niagara.edu

Paul Smith's College of Arts and Science
Hospitality Management
paulsmiths.edu

Rochester Institute of Technology
School of Food and Hotel Management
rit.edu

Schenectady County Community College
Department of Hotel, Culinary Arts, and Tourism
sunysccc.edu

State University of New York College, Buffalo
   (Buffalo State College)
Food Systems Management
Faculty of Applied Science and Education
Nutrition and Food Science Department
buffalostate.edu

State University of New York, Cobleskill
Foodservice and Hospitality Management
cobleskill.edu

State University of New York College, Plattsburgh
Hotel and Restaurant Management
Center for Human Resources
http://www2.plattsburgh.edu

Suffolk County Community College
Hotel, Restaurant Management
sunysuffolk.edu

Sullivan County Community College
Hospitality Management
sullivan.suny.edu

Syracuse University
Restaurant and Foodservice Management Program
College for Human Development
Department of Nutrition and Foodservice Management
http://chd.syr.edu

Tompkins Cortland Community College
Hospitality, Business, and Public Service Division
sunytccc.edu

Trocaire College
Hospitality Management
trocaire.edu

Villa Maria College
Hospitality Management
villa.edu

## *North Carolina*

Alamance Community College
Foodservice Management
alamance.cc.nc.us

Asheville-Buncombe Technical Community College
Hotel/Restaurant Management
asheville.cc.nc.us

Cape Fear Community College
Hotel/Restaurant Management
cfcc.edu

Central Piedmont Community College
Hospitality Education
cpcc.cc.nc.us

Fayetteville Technical Community College
Foodservice Management
faytech.cc.nc.us

Guilford Technical Community College, Jamestown Campus
Culinary Arts Technology
http://technet.gtcc.cc.nc.us

Lenoir Community College
Foodservice Management
lenoir.cc.nc.us

North Carolina Central University
Hospitality Services Management Program
Department of Home Economics
http://web.nccu.edu

North Carolina State University
ces.ncsu.edu

North Carolina Wesleyan College
Restaurant Management
ncwc.edu

Robeson Community College
Culinary Technology
robeson.cc.nc.us

Sandhills Community College
Hotel and Restaurant Management
sandhills.cc.nc.us

Southwestern Community College
Hospitality Services
southwest.cc.nc.us

University of North Carolina at Greensboro
Department of Nutrition
uncg.edu

Wake Technical Community College
Hotel, Restaurant Management, and Culinary Arts
wake.tec.nc.us

Wilkes Community College
Hotel/Restaurant/Foodservice Management
wilkes.cc.nc.us

## *North Dakota*

Bismarck State College
Hotel, Restaurant Management
bsc.nodak.edu

North Dakota State College of Science
Culinary Arts Department
ndscs.nodak.edu

North Dakota State University
Hotel, Motel, Restaurant Management Program
College of Human Development and Education
ndsu.edu

## *Ohio*

Bluffton College
Food and Nutrition—Dietetics
bluffton.edu

Bowling Green State University
Hospitality Management Program
Business Administration
cba.bgsu.edu

Cincinnati Technical College
Hospitality Management
cinstate.cc.oh.us

Columbus State Community College
Hospitality Management
http://cscc.edu

Cuyahoga Community College
Hospitality Management
tri-c.cc.oh.us

Hocking College
Hotel, Restaurant Management/Culinary Arts
hocking.edu

Kent State University
Hospitality, Food Service Management
School of Family and Consumer Studies
http://dept.kent.edu

Muskingum Tech
Culinary Arts
matc.tec.oh.us

Ohio University
Food Service Management and Dietetics
School of Human and Consumer Sciences
ohio.edu

Sinclair Community College
Hospitality Management
sinclair.edu

The University of Akron
Community and Technical College
Hospitality Management
commtech.uakron.edu

University of Findlay
Hospitality Management
findlay.edu

Western Reserve School of Cooking
wrsoc.com

## *Oklahoma*

Meridian Technology Center
Culinary Arts
meridian-technology.com

Oklahoma State University, Okmulgee
Foodservice Management, Culinary Arts
osu-okmulgee.edu

Oklahoma State University, Stillwater
School of Hotel and Restaurant Administration
College of Human Environmental Sciences
http://ches.okstate.edu

Pioneer Technical Center
Foodservices
pioneertech.org

## *Oregon*

Central Oregon Community College
Hotel, Restaurant Management
cocc.edu

Chemeketa Community College
Hospitality Management
chemek.cc.or.us

International School of Baking
Culinary Arts
schoolofbaking.com

Lane Community College
Foodservice Management
http://lanecc.edu

Mt. Hood Community College
Hospitality and Tourism Management
mhcc.cc.or.us

Oregon State University
Hotel, Restaurant, and Tourism
hhs.oregonstate.edu

Portland State University
Food Industry Leadership Center
foodleadership.pdx.edu

Southern Oregon University
Hotel, Restaurant, and Resort Management
Option School of Business
sou.edu

Southwestern Oregon Community College
Oregon Coast Culinary Institute
socc.edu

Western Culinary Institute
Le Cordon Bleu Culinary Program
westernculinary.com

## *Pennsylvania*

The Art Institute of Philadelphia
Culinary Arts
aiph.artinstitutes.edu

Bucks County Community College
Hospitality, Tourism, Food Service Management
bucks.edu

Community College of Allegheny County, Boyce Campus
Hospitality Management
ccac.edu

Delaware Community College
Hotel-Restaurant Management
dccc.edu

Delaware Valley College
Food Science and Management
http://campus.devalcol.edu

Drexel University
Department of Hotel, Restaurant, and Institutional Management
drexel.edu

East Stroudsburg University
Hotel, Restaurant, and Tourism Management
esu.edu

Harrisburg Area Community College
Hospitality and Tourism
hacc.edu

Indiana University of Pennsylvania
Academy of Culinary Arts
iup.edu

Keystone Junior College
Hotel, Restaurant, and Food Service Management/Travel and
   Tourism
keystone.edu

Luzerne County Community College
Hotel, Restaurant, and Institutional Management
luzerne.edu

Mansfield University
Nutrition Programs
mnsfld.edu

Marywood University
Hospitality Management
marywood.edu

Northampton Community College
Hotel/Restaurant Management/Culinary Arts
northampton.edu

Pennsylvania College of Technology
Food and Hospitality and Culinary Arts
http://www2.pct.edu

Pennsylvania Culinary Institute
Culinary Arts
paculinary.com

The Pennsylvania State University
Hotel, Restaurant, and Recreation Management
college.sccm.cc.ne.us

The Restaurant School
Culinary Arts
therestaurantschool.com

Robert Morris University
Hospitality Management
robert-morris.edu

Temple University
School of Tourism and Hospitality Management
temple.edu

Westmoreland County Community College
Hospitality Management
http://www2.westmoreland.cc.pa.us

## *Rhode Island*

Johnson and Wales University
College of Culinary Arts
jwu.edu

University of Rhode Island
Department of Nutrition and Food Sciences
uri.edu

## *South Carolina*

Clemson University
Department of Parks, Recreation, and Tourism
clemson.edu

College of Charleston
Hospitality and Tourism Management
cofc.edu

Garrett Academy of Technology
Culinary Arts
garrettacademy.org

Greenville Technical College
Foodservice Management
greenvilletech.com

Horry Georgetown Technical College
Hospitality and Tourism Management
hor.tec.sc.us

Johnson and Wales University at Charleston
Hospitality Program
jwu.edu/hosp/index.htm

Spartanburg Technical College
Hospitality Management
spt.tec.sc.us

Trident Technical College
Hospitality/Tourism Management
tridenttech.org

University of South Carolina
School of Hotel, Restaurant, and Tourism Administration
Applied Professional Sciences
hrsm.sc.edu

Winthrop College
Nutrition
Department of Human Nutrition
winthrop.edu

## *South Dakota*

Black Hills State University
Travel Industry Management
College of Business and Public Affairs
bhsu.edu

Mitchell Technical Institute
Culinary Arts
http://mti.tec.sd.us

South Dakota State University
Nutrition and Food Science Department
http://www3.sdstate.edu

## *Tennessee*

Belmont College
Hospitality Business
http://schlbus.belmont.edu

Opryland Hotel Culinary Institute
http://members.tripod.com/~culinaryclassics/ohci.html

Pellissippi State Technical Community College
Hospitality
pstcc.cc.tn.us

Tennessee State University
Hotel and Restaurant Administration
tnstate.edu

The University of Tennessee, Knoxville
Hotel and Restaurant Administration
http://web.utk.edu

Volunteer State Community College
Hotel and Restaurant Management
http://www2.volstate.edu

Walters State Community College
Hotel and Restaurant Management
wscc.cc.tn.us

## *Texas*

The Art Institute of Dallas
http://aid.artinstitutes.edu

The Art Institute of Houston
Culinary Arts
aih.aii.edu

Austin Community College
Hospitality Management
http://www2.austin.cc.tx.us/hospmgmt

Central Texas College
Hospitality Management
ctcd.cc.tx.us

Culinary Academy of Austin
culinaryacademyofaustin.com

Del Mar College
Hospitality Management
delmar.edu

Galveston College
Culinary Arts
gc.edu

North Lake College
Hospitality Management
northlakecollege.edu

Odessa College
Culinary Arts
odessa.edu

St. Philip's College
Tourism, Hospitality, and Culinary Arts
accd.edu/spc/spcmain/spc.htm

South Texas Community College
Hospitality and Tourism, Culinary Arts
stcc.cc.tx.us

Texas Culinary Academy
txca.com

Texas State Technical Institute
Foodservice and Culinary Arts
waco.tstc.edu

Texas Tech University
Restaurant, Hotel, and Institutional Management
College of Human Services
Nutrition and Restaurant/Hotel Management
hs.ttu.edu

University of Houston
Hotel and Restaurant Management
Conrad N. Hilton College of Hotel and Restaurant Management
hrm.uh.edu

University of North Texas
Hospitality Management
unt.edu

## *Utah*

Bridgerland Applied Technology Center
Nutrition and Food
batc.tec.ut.us

Salt Lake Community College
Culinary Arts
slcc.edu

Utah State University
Department of Nutrition and Food Sciences
usu.edu

Utah Valley State College
Hospitality Management
uvsc.edu

## *Vermont*

Champlain College
Hotel, Restaurant Management
champlain.edu

Johnson State College
Hotel, Hospitality Management
johnsonstatecollege.edu

New England Culinary Institute
Culinary Arts
neculinary.com

University of Vermont
Nutrition and Food Sciences
http://nutrition.uvm.edu

## *Virginia*

Dabney S. Lancaster Community College
Hospitality Management, Culinary Arts
dl.cc.va.us

J. Sargeant Reynolds Community College
The School of Culinary Arts, Tourism, and Hospitality
jsr.vccs.edu

James Madison University
Hotel-Restaurant Management Department
College of Business
jmu.edu

Johnson and Wales University
Culinary Arts
jwu.edu

Northern Virginia Community College
Hotel, Restaurant, and Institutional Management
nv.cc.va.us

Radford University
Foodservice Management
runet.edu

Southwest Virginia Community College
Hospitality
sw.vccs.edu

Stratford University
Hospitality, Culinary Arts
stratford.edu

Tidewater Community College
Hotel, Restaurant, and Institutional Management
tc.cc.va.us

Virginia Polytechnic Institute and State University
Hospitality and Tourism Management
cob.vt.edu

Wytheville Community College
Hospitality Industry Management
wc.cc.va.us

## *Washington*

The Art Institute of Seattle
Culinary Arts
ais.edu

Bellingham Technical College
Culinary Arts
btc.ctc.edu

Clark College
Culinary Arts/Restaurant Management
clark.edu

Clover Park Technical College
Restaurant Management
cptc.ctc.edu

Edmonds Community College
Culinary Arts
http://careers.edcc.edu

Highline Community College
Hotel and Tourism Management Program
http://flightline.highline.edu

North Seattle Community College
Culinary Arts
northseattle.edu

Pierce College
Restaurant Management
pierce.ctc.edu

Renton Technical College
Culinary Arts
renton-tc.ctc.edu

Seattle Central Community College
Hospitality and Culinary Arts
seattlecentral.org

Skagit Valley College
Foodservice Management
skagit.edu

South Puget Sound Community College
Culinary Arts
spscc.ctc.edu

South Seattle Community College
Culinary Arts
chefschool.com

Spokane Community College
Hotel, Motel, Restaurant Management
scc.spokane.cc.wa.us

Walla Walla Community College
wwcc.edu

Washington State University
Hospitality Business Management
College of Business and Economics
wsu.edu

## *West Virginia*

Concord College
Travel Industry Management
concord.wvnet.edu

Mountain State University
Hospitality Management, Culinary Arts
mountainstate.edu

West Virginia Northern Community College
Culinary Arts
http://techctr1.northern.wvnet.edu

West Virginia University
Restaurant/Food Service Management
College of Agriculture and Forestry
caf.wvu.edu

## *Wisconsin*

Blackhawk Technical College
Culinary Arts
blackhawk.edu

Chippewa Valley Technical College
Hospitality and Tourism Management, Culinary Arts
chippewa.tec.wi.us

Fox Valley Technical College
Culinary Arts
fvtc.edu

Madison Area Technical College
Hospitality Management
http://matcmadison.edu

Mid-State Technical College
Hotel/Restaurant Management
http://midstate.tec.wi.us

Milwaukee Area Technical College
Culinary Arts
http://oncampus.matc.edu

Moraine Park Technical College
Culinary Arts
moraine.tec.wi.us

Nicolet Area Technical College
Hospitality Management, Culinary Art
nicolet.tec.wi.us

University of Wisconsin, Madison
Department of Nutritional Sciences
wisc.edu

University of Wisconsin, Stout
Hospitality and Tourism Management
School of Home Economics
uwstout.edu

Waukesha County Technical College
Hospitality Management, Culinary Arts
waukesha.tec.wi.us

## *Wyoming*

Sheridan College
Hospitality Management Program
sc.cc.wy.us

University of Wyoming
General Dietetics
College of Agriculture
uwyo.edu

# Canadian Schools Offering Hospitality Programs

## *Alberta*

Southern Alberta Institute of Technology
Hotel and Restaurant Management
adpu-uae.com/partners/sait/index.htm

## *British Columbia*

Camosun College
Hotel/Restaurant Administration
camosun.bc.ca/schools/index.php

Malaspina University College
Hospitality Management
mala.ca/index.asp

## *Manitoba*

Red River College
Hotel and Restaurant Administration
rrc.mb.ca

## *Newfoundland*

Westviking College of Applied Arts, Technology, and Continuing
    Education
Hotel and Restaurant Management
westvikingc.nf.ca

## *Ontario*

Algonquin College
Hotel and Restaurant Management
algonquinc.on.ca/highband/swf/index.htm

Cambrian College
Hotel and Restaurant Management
cambrianc.on.ca

Canadore College
Hotel, Resort, and Restaurant Management
canadorec.on.ca

Confederation College
Hotel Management
confederationc.on.ca

Fanshawe College
Hotel and Restaurant Management
fanshawec.on.ca

George Brown College
Hotel Management
gbrownc.on.ca

Humber College
Hotel and Restaurant Management
humberc.on.ca

Loyalist College
Hotel and Restaurant Management
loyalistc.on.ca

Niagara College
Hotel and Restaurant Administration
niagarac.on.ca

Saint Clair College
Hotel Management
stclairc.on.ca

Saint Lawrence College
Hotel and Restaurant Management
stlawrencec.on.ca

Sault College
Hotel and Restaurant Management
saultc.on.ca

## *Prince Edward Island*

Holland College
Hospitality Management
hollandc.pe.ca

## *Quebec*

College Lasalle (French language school)
Hotel Management Techniques
clasalle.qc.ca

Concordia University
Tourism and Hospitality Management
http://search.concordia.ca

## *Saskatchewan*

Kelsey Institute
Hotel and Restaurant Administration
siast.sk.ca/kelsey

## Appendix C

# *Food Industry Associations*

THE FOLLOWING IS a list of associations to contact for further information on opportunities in restaurant careers:

American Culinary Federation
10 San Bartola Dr.
St. Augustine, FL 32086
acfchefs.org

The American Dietetic Association
120 S. Riverside Plaza, Ste. 2000
Chicago, IL 60606
eatright.org

The American Hotel and Lodging Association
1201 New York Ave. NW
Washington, DC 20005
ahla.com

Culinary Institute of America
1946 Campus Dr.
Hyde Park, NY 12538
ciachef.edu

Dietary Managers Association
406 Surrey Woods Dr.
St. Charles, IL 60174
dmaonline.org

International Council on Hotel, Restaurant, and
    Institutional Education
2613 N. Parham Rd.
Richmond, VA 23294
infor@chrie.org

National Restaurant Association Educational Foundation
175 W. Jackson Blvd., Ste. 1500
Chicago, IL 60604
nraef.org

National Restaurant Association Information Service and Library
1200 Seventeenth St. NW
Washington, DC 20036
restaurant.org

Good sources of information also include local employers, your individual state employment services, any of the schools listed in Appendixes A and B, and trade periodicals such as the following:

*Dietary Manager Magazine*
406 Surrey Woods Dr.
St. Charles, IL 60174
dmaonline.org

*Food Management*
1300 E. Ninth St.
Cleveland, OH 44114
foodservicesearch.com

*Lodging Magazine*
1201 New York Ave. NW, Ste. 600
Washington, DC 20005
ahla.com

*National Culinary Review*
10 Bartola Dr.
St. Augustine, FL 32086
acfchefs.org

*Nation's Restaurant News*
425 Park Ave.
New York, NY 10017
nrn.com

*Restaurant Business*
770 Broadway
New York, NY 10003
restaurantbiz.com

*Restaurants and Institutions*
Cahners Plaza
1350 Touhy Ave.
P.O. Box 5080
Des Plaines, IL 60017
rimag.com

*Restaurants USA*
1201 Seventeenth St. NW
Washington, DC 20036
restaurant.org

# ABOUT THE AUTHOR

CAROL ANN CAPRIONE CHMELYNSKI began her food-service career in 1976 with the National Milk Producers Federation. She went on to become an editorial assistant at the Food Marketing Institute and later worked as a communications specialist at the National Restaurant Association in Washington, D.C., where she wrote feature articles for the association's monthly magazine, *NR,4 News*. That magazine is now titled *Restaurants USA*.

Mrs. Chmelynski worked as a copywriter for the advertising firm of Stackig, Sanderson, and White in McLean, Virginia, where she wrote product as well as job recruitment ads for high-technology companies such as Electronic Data Systems, Network Solutions, Tempest Technologies, and Capital Systems Group, Incorporated.

Currently Mrs. Chmelynski is the assistant managing editor of *School Board News*, a biweekly newspaper of the National School Boards Association in Alexandria, Virginia.

*Opportunities in Restaurant Careers* is Mrs. Chmelynski's second book in the VGM Career Books series. Her first book, *Opportunities in Food Service Careers*, was published in 1992.